Bernadette Vallely has been inte[rested in ...] and the occult since she was a te[enager. Her] work on social activism started w[ith ... the] Anti-Nazi League, the Campaign [...] and the Anti-Apartheid Movemen[t ... Friends of] the Earth in the 1980s and it resulted in her setting up and becoming Director of the Women's Environmental Network until 1994. She is author of many books including the bestselling *Young Person's Guide to Saving the Planet* (Virago, 1990) and *1001 Ways to Save the Planet* (Penguin, 1990). She lives in London with her husband Stewart and daughter Alexandria. She is a clairvoyant medium.

The Young Person's Guide to

Mind, Body and Spirit

Bernadette Vallely

Published by VIRAGO PRESS Limited, August 1994
42–43 Gloucester Crescent, London NW1 7PD

Copyright © Bernadette Vallely

The right of Bernadette Vallely to be identified
as author of this work has been asserted by her
in accordance with the Copyright.
Designs and Patents Act 1988.

All rights reserved

*A CIP catalogue record for this book
is available from the British Library*

Typeset by CentraCet, Cambridge
Printed in Great Britain by Cox & Wyman Ltd, Reading, Berks

In loving memory of Annie Russell Jones

IMPORTANT NOTICE

The publishers and the author wish to state that there are many psychic practices, including the misuse of herbs and oils, communicating with discarnate entities, certain types of meditation, astral travelling, misuse of hypnotism and similar practices that can cause sickness, poison the body, cause hallucinations, short-term and long-term emotional and physical illness, and in rare cases death. If you are in any doubt about your personal safety or the safety of others, you have a responsibility to consult a reputable specialist. The publishers and the author cannot accept any responsibility for any damage suffered from the use of any psychic or spiritual practice included in this book.

Acknowledgements

Many people have helped with this publication, from the authors of the marvellous books that have guided me to my understanding of the complex subjects covered to the teachers and spirit guides that have offered understanding and support when I needed it, and I thank them all.

I especially want to thank Orla Fox who has operated the computer with lightness and laughter and to whom I owe many hours of gratitude. For all those people who read and commented on the manuscript, taught me much, and offered positive feedback and enthusiasm including Melanie Silgardo, Tony Neate, Helen O'Hara, Sabrina Dearborn, William Bloom, Chris Russell Jones, James Bloom, Francesca and Roberta Jaggs, Carin Lowenborg, Isobel Hudson, Anna Jaskolka, Suzzane Quinney, the staff and librarian at the College of Psychic Studies, Felicity Aldridge, Caitlin Matthews, and my family who have supported me and loved me through this long process, my husband and friend Stewart and my daughter Alexandria, who I hope will benefit from the book in years to come.

To write to the author

Letters to the author are very welcome, especially if they contain stories about your meetings with angels, ghosts or similar. We appreciate hearing from you and learning of your enjoyment of this book. Please always enclose a stamped addressed envelope (or an international postal reply coupon if you are writing from outside the UK) if you want a reply to your letter although we cannot guarantee that every letter can be answered. Please write to:

Bernadette Vallely
PO Box 3724
London, N16 6HY

Contents

Introduction xi

affirmations 1
alchemy 2
amulets 3
angels 4
apparitions 6
astral travelling 7
astrology 9
aura 11
automatic writing 14
black magic 16
breath 17
buddhism 18
candles 21
chakras 21
channelling 24
chanting 27
clairvoyance 28
crystals and precious stones 30
death 33
déjà vu 36
divination 37
dowsing 38
dreams 40

druids 44
earth magic 46
earth mysteries and markings 48
etheric body 50
exorcism 51
fairies 54
festivals 57
Gaia 62
ghosts 63
gods and goddesses 64
guardian angels or guides 65
gurus 67
healing 68
herbs 70
higher self 73
hypnosis 74
I Ching 76
incense and oils 78
Jesus 81
Jung 82
karma 84
ley lines 85
magic 87
meditation 89

mediums 91
myths and legends, folk tales and fables 94
near death experiences 96
new age 98
numerology 99
occult 103
ouija board 103
out-of-body experiences 104
paganism 107
palmistry 108
parapsychology 110
past lives 111
pendulum power 112
personal growth 114
poltergeists 116
protection 118
psychic 120
psychokinesis 122
psychometry 125
qabalah 126
reincarnation 128
religion and religious beliefs 131
rituals 134
runes 135

sacred stones 138
sceptics 140
scrying 142
shamanism 144
spiritualism 145
superstitions 146
taoism 148
tarot cards 149
telepathy 151
third eye 152
unidentified flying objects (UFOs) 154
unconditional love 156
vampires 158
visualisation 160
voodoo 163
werewolves 165
witches and witchcraft 166
yoga 169
zen 171

Short booklist 172
Bookshops 173
Magazines 174
Addresses to contact 176
Books to read 181

Introduction

So what happens if you see a ghost? Hear strange noises in the night? What exactly is a ouija board? What would you do if you had an ESP experience or if you went astral travelling? Or talked to a medium? These are all considered to be psychic experiences and a growing number of people in Britain, especially when young, claim to have had them at some point in their lives.

The problem with psychic experiences is that they stop being psychic when science can identify them and explain them. Even so there are a large number of unanswered questions and riddles that science, even after many years, has been unable to solve. Such as: what is the origin of the Stonehenge circle, and how did people erect such a huge monument, which would have been very difficult, even by today's standards? And how do so many people continuously recount similar stories regarding near death and out-of-body experiences? How do children tell us accurately of past lives in different towns and countries when they are only five years old? How can people tell so much about your character from reading tarot cards, or the palms of your hand? How can you answer questions that puzzle you by throwing I Ching coins?

These experiences are important to all of us. They have been told and retold, experienced and re-experienced over thousands of years. In some societies people who can see the future, who can read cards or explain unusual dreams, are considered healers and shámans or spiritual people and they are treated with reverence. In modern Western society our obsession with science as the basis of all truth has left us largely bereft of a spiritual or mystical past that we believe in, or a spiritual future that we want to see and experience ourselves.

When you open yourself up to psychic and spiritual phenomena you will find it an immensely rewarding and magical process. Once you've seen one angel you can see thousands, but only if you continue to believe in them. If you want to monitor scientifically the existence of angels you will find it very difficult, but in the meantime you will miss the experience – what a waste!

This book has been written for those who need straightforward explanations about strange phenomena, for people who are willing to explore another part of their minds and get in touch with their souls. It is a book for young people who want to start to live magically in the twenty-first century, and prepare for the New Age of Aquarius that is almost upon us. It is a book for young people who want to rid themselves of the narrow-mindedness that still believes that witches are evil, that life after death doesn't exist and that you can't have a conversation with a spirit or an angel.

If you have had a spiritual or psychic experience, this book is for you. You can learn about psychic protection and safety. You can learn some of the deeper, more spiritual explanations about spirit guides, fairies and angels. And you can learn to expand your consciousness to embrace the future with new skills and experiences. If it works for you – do it! Become an optimystic!

Bernadette Vallely
March 1994

Affirmations

Affirmations are positive magic. To tell yourself that you can achieve your goals increases your chances of attaining those goals by a high margin. Positive affirmations change your old ideas and beliefs about yourself and create a new inner symbolism that you can follow.

For instance, suppose you have a belief system that says to yourself, 'Life is hard' or, 'I am unlucky' or even, 'I never get anywhere', you are literally telling your conscious and subconscious self that you believe this to be true, and your whole body accepts it. Pretty soon you don't have to believe it because it will be happening to you in reality. You have created and drawn towards you those situations which you fear!

If you say to yourself, as often as you can, 'Life is good', 'I enjoy my life' and, 'I am healthy' or, 'I can do anything I want to do' then you will be using affirmations to destroy the negative myths created in your mind and reprogram new ones. Expect a miracle to happen, every day – and it will!

■ *What you can do*

Write down the old beliefs and myths that you have about yourself and then write down new, positive ones. Tear up the old ones and repeat the new every day, think about them, feel them, visualise them, write them down, like lines, again and again. Become an OPTIMYSTIC! Do things for pleasure. Enjoy what's going on around you and more of the same will come your way. Read *Living Magically*, by Gill Edwards (Piatkus, 1991) and *Illusions: the Adventures of a Reluctant Messiah*, by Richard Bach (Pan Books, 1977).

Alchemy

Alchemy is, without doubt, the first natural science studied and it gave way to the early forms of chemistry and other sciences. All knowledge, of metals and gold, or reincarnation and sexual reproduction, of immortality and unknown mysteries were connected in early civilisations with mysticism. After all, as an esoteric science (esoteric means secretly handed down by word of mouth, always involving information that is mystic) the art of alchemy attracted many men and women who would be the philosophers and scientists of today's modern world.

There are many versions of the origin of the word 'alchemy'. Some say the word derived from the Arabic and means 'matter of Egypt' or 'the knowledge of Egyptian Art' or 'the magical craft of the black country'. Others believe it comes from the Greek word *chemeia*, which means the transmutation of gold and silver. Wherever the word derived from originally, the study of alchemy quickly began to encompass lessons and writings on pharmacy, astrology, philosophy, metallurgy, herbalism and 'magical incantations'.

One of the earliest quests of the alchemist was the search for everlasting life, or immortality. Through this search much work was done to unravel some of the secrets of reincarnation and the immortality of the soul itself.

The alchemists' basic idea was that every metal contained varying proportions of the four elements – earth, air, fire and water – and that if you could understand in exactly which proportions these elements were to be found in gold and silver then you could duplicate the effect and transform ordinary metals like copper into gold. The idea was alluring, of course, and many wealthy people lost fortunes funding laboratories that were supposedly able to make gold and bring enlightenment to the soul at the same time.

The scientists had to carry out their art in secrecy during the Inquisition, as everyone carrying out such practices could be tortured or worse, burnt at the stake as a witch and heretic. Because of this much of the language and detail of the alchemists' work was hidden in secret texts, so obscure that their meaning and nature was hidden from the inquisitors and anyone not seriously interested in the subject.

■ *What you can do*

Modern alchemy is studied as new science and metaphysics. The most interesting work that connects the spiritual and the scientific worlds includes Rupert Sheldrake's theory on morphic resonance outlined in *The Presence of the Past: Morphic Resonance and the Habits of Nature* (Collins, 1988) and other books exploring the nature of communication, chaos and complexity of the cosmos. For a good all-round description of alchemy as a spiritual and historical art read *Alchemy* by Cherry Gilchrist (Element, 1991), *The Lure and Romance of Alchemy*, by C. J. S. Thompson (Bell Publishing) and *Alchemy: The Medieval Alchemists and their Royal Art*, by Johannes Fabricius (Aquarian, 1989).

Amulets

An amulet is the name given to jewellery, clothing or any other object used by the Egyptians to protect the body, whether it was alive or dead, from evil influences of a human or a spiritual nature. It is broadly used to denote any kind of ornament to which magic and occult powers are given.

In Egyptian history the amulet seems to have been first worn to protect the bearer from wild animals, but over several generations amulets became an important part of the protection of the dead. The earliest type of amulet found on the dead in Egypt consists of small pieces of green schist, a beautiful precious stone, which were always laid on the heart of the person to be buried. The words spoken to energise the amulet were known as *hekau*, or 'words of power'.

Other religions and beliefs also use amulets – rings of power, crosses, crystals, tapestry vestments, necklaces, etc. Many prayers and rituals included amulets so that the objects could be energised with the necessary power to protect the owner.

Modern amulets include crystals and handmade jewellery, and they are widely available.

■ *What you can do*

Visit the British Museum and similar museums, which often have examples of early amulets on display. Look especially in Egyptian history for clues to the use of these items. What can you use today? You can make your own amulet for personal use and protection by choosing an appropriate piece, cleansing it with salt water and preparing your own ritual over it. See RITUALS, MAGIC.

Angels

Beings of beautiful light, angels, have been in our history since time began. They are said to represent an essence of human form, although they are usually seen with a human-like body and wings. The poet William Blake saw angels when he was a small boy and was severely beaten by his father for saying so. In 1985 on a trip to the moon, six Russian cosmonauts claim that they saw angels as 'seven giant figures in the form of humans, but with wings. They appeared to be hundreds of feet tall with a wingspan as great as a jetliner'. One cosmonaut described the angels as surrounded by a bright orange light which temporarily blinded them and they were all overwhelmed with the beauty and smiles of these beings. They didn't believe what they saw at first but these beautiful creatures stayed around them for several days. All the cosmonauts experienced these angels. They wrote a report which was suppressed by the Kremlin for many years but smuggled out of Russia and released to the press only a few years ago.

Angels have been seen by hundreds of thousands of men and women, depicted by great artists, written about by poets, writers and thinkers. In 1991 the Pope declared to the world's press that 'angels exist, they are sentient beings who have come to earth to help us'.

Indeed, anyone who has seen angels and has been touched by the sheer brilliance of their light, the calmness of their manner and the help that they offer without reward cannot fail to be impressed. They are also said to be responsible for bringing messages of hope as well as news of the deaths of relatives and loved ones. They are not, however, the same as ghosts or spirits, as angels have never incarnated, or lived, as a human being with flesh.

No one can really know exactly where an angel comes from but it is clear that they exist in a form not easily or obviously visible to the majority of people on earth. It is highly unlikely that they are connected to any one religion as most religions, even the most obscure, have reports and stories about them. The best explanation is that they exist on another 'frequency' or 'vibration' of energy to our very dense, physical one, and their light and goodness make it likely that they have religious connections. This other frequency is often called the 'other world' or the 'spirit kingdom'.

There are said to be angels ready and able to help humans and all forms of life, connecting their special 'energy' to ours in order to perceive and encourage the best possible light and goodness that is available. Angels also exist in a kind of order that is graded according to their ability and light and experience, so there are ordinary everyday angels that help with little things like lost valuables, or when people are upset, and you can pretty much call on them all the time to help you when you need it. Other angels hold responsibility and awareness for whole areas, villages and towns, even for cities and countries. These 'overlighting angels' are also responsible for helping other beings like fairies and devas with nature and natural events. (See FAIRIES.)

There are angels and archangels on many realms living in harmony with the rest of life on our planet earth. So many people have seen them, in so many countries, that the fact that anyone can still disbelieve in these heavenly creatures is just a sad representation of how we have dissociated ourselves from these other worlds.

In Findhorn, a spiritual centre in Northern Scotland, there is an overlighting angel called the Angel of Findhorn who has been seen by many and has offered hope and love when people needed it. One young woman there was very depressed about certain things that had happened between herself and her mother. She sat up all night crying about it when an angel came to her and opened its wings and they were full of the most beautiful flowers she had ever seen. Somehow this helped her deep inside and things started to look better for her. Findhorn is also the place where Angel Cards were invented; these are tiny pictures of angels with words like 'creativity', 'abundance', 'joy', and 'truth' on them. You are invited to pick a card, and when you see the word that is written with the angel, you 'invite' that angel into your life at that time. Although it can be treated as just a game, the cards picked can often have deep and definite meaning for people.

■ *What you can do*

Start to get in touch with angels by asking them to help with little things that go wrong; if you lose something, for instance, or when you are very sad. Ask for help and thank them when you find it. Meditation often helps you to 'see' angels too.

Ask around. Have any of your friends spotted these beautiful creatures? You may be surprised that people feel too embarrassed to talk about angels, often not believing themselves or their own eyes until others start the conversation first.

Look out for angels in paintings and in other forms of art and history; there are many more than you realise.

Get hold of Angel Cards from Findhorn (see ADDRESSES TO CONTACT and try them with your friends.

Read *Commune with the Angels: A Heavenly Handbook*, by Jane M. Howard (ARE Press, 1992); *Ask Your Angels*, by Alma Daniel, Timothy Wyllie and Andrew Ramer (Ballantine Books, 1992); *A Book of Angels*, by Sophy Burnham (Ballantine Books, 1990); and *Meetings with Angels: A Hundred and One Real-life Encounters*, by H. C. Moolenburgh (C. W. Daniel, 1992).

See FAIRIES, MEDITATION.

Apparitions

It is estimated that about half of the population have experienced apparitions of some description or another. These are usually astral 'leftovers' from people who have died or even ghosts who walk on earth who are perhaps disturbed and haven't found the 'other side', or the spiritual realms.

■ *What you can do*

If you see an apparition don't panic! Panicking and fear can give the being more of your energy, which in turn makes it more energised and powerful and so more people will see it. Ask your guide, or guardian angel, to help you to send the apparition 'on to the light'. This step will ease the situation and you can be sure you are doing something positive.

See GHOSTS, GUARDIAN ANGELS, GUIDES.

Astral Plane

The astral plane exists as another reality. It operates as another world which is one stage removed from our dense, physical one. This is the first of the planes or worlds that the body goes to upon death and is the plane that is usually travelled to in astral travelling, linking the ordinary world and images and happenings with our subconscious. It can be the place where the dead stay without wanting to move on to other realms. They then become ghosts.

The astral plane works on our emotional level and is dominated by our emotional thoughts which can, in turn, become our reality. Just look at where our fantasies of science fiction, horror stories and other fantasy movies come from.

See ASTRAL TRAVELLING, OUT-OF-BODY EXPERIENCES, ETHERIC BODY, DEATH, GHOSTS.

Astral Travelling

Travelling out from your physical body to other places and other worlds has been known and revered in cultures and societies for thousands of years. The Native American Indians used astral travelling to greet ancestors and also the living. In Mexico, Africa, Egypt, Australia and the Indian subcontinent stories of people travelling in their sleep are recounted continuously through history.

One South African writer, Peter Richelieu, has recorded in his work *A Soul's Journey*, how he was taught to astral travel by an Indian mystic who wanted to show him the different levels of being and reality. He travelled not just to various cities on earth, like London and Tokyo, but also to various realms in space where he met angels and spirits who had died many years previously.

Common agreement on how astral travelling works centres around the physical body separating from the astral or etheric body, usually during sleep, although both bodies are connected by a cord.

The businessman and psychic Robert Monroe had his first out-of-body experience in 1958 and he began to record in notebooks all his astral journeys after he learnt from friends that yogis and practitioners of other Eastern religions seemed to be able to travel at will. Monroe claims he visited three different dimensions, which he called locales. Locale I he describes as the Astral Plane (see ASTRAL PLANE). In locale II, beyond this world, time and space were unreal. Locale III he described as a bizarre double world where identical life went on but technology was different, with the inhabitants relying on a form of energy that was invisible.

■ *What you can do*

Monroe was eager for others to try astral travelling themselves, but his guidelines are difficult and unclear. If you do find yourself travelling, even without trying, you should make sure you can focus on your physical body in order to get back into this world or you could be in serious difficulties. Astral travelling is *not* recommended to the uninitiated by many of the best psychics in Britain because so many people get into trouble.

When travelling in the astral plane you may well enter worlds that are strange and mysterious and you could meet people who travel in their astral bodies, ghosts or spirits who are extremely dangerous. The best way to protect yourself from this is to be very clear, even to the point of verbalising it in ritual, that you wish only to travel to realms and places that you are ready and able to handle and you must ensure that you will be protected and safe at all times. Include your guides and ask guardian angels to help you.

See also PROTECTION, ETHERIC BODY, ASTRAL PLANE, RITUALS, OUT-OF-BODY EXPERIENCES.

Astrology

The ancient science of astrology is more complex than the sun star columns that you read in newspapers and magazines. Yet our fascination with such matters has allowed the modern media to reduce us all to the two sentences found in a daily newspaper column. The bit that we all tend to know is the zodiac sign the sun was in when we were born – Aries, Scorpio, Capricorn, etc. – but real astrology goes much further and is, of course, a complex science.

Astrology originated in Mesopotamia, part of the country we now call Iraq, and was practised by people who were forecasters and interpreters of omens. They had watched women use the cycles of the moon to plant and harvest grain and vegetables and they knew that the moon cycles were important times when it was either good or unlucky to carry out ventures. Proof has been found that during the fifth century BC and nineteenth century AD astrologers recognised thousands of omens regarding the planets and their alignments, eclipses, stars, and their positions and times.

Many astrologers were skilled in the sciences of astronomy and philosophy and it is this varied mixture which gives astrology its edge as a specialist form of divination, or fortune-telling.

Astrology in its various forms has been used by many famous and wealthy people all over the world. Revelations that the former President of the United States, Ronald Reagan, didn't do anything important without consulting his wife's astrologer caused a sensation in the 1980s, but he was by no means the first major politician to consult this form of divination for help. St Thomas Aquinas respected astrology, claiming that 'man's fate is the power exerted by the stars and their movements', and Pope Julius II planned the date of his coronation by the stars. Pope Leo X is said to have founded the first chair of astrology in a university, and the Church at the time, eager to get the respect it needed, associated signs of the zodiac with various apostles. Protestants were not as enamoured of the art as were Catholics, and Queen Elizabeth I imposed legal penalties against anyone who dared to cast a horoscope for royalty.

There are many uses of astrology today. The most common is in horoscopes which are cast according to the time of birth. The horoscope is an astronomically accurate diagram of the positions of the sun, moon, Mercury, Venus, Mars, Jupiter, Saturn, Uranus, Neptune and Pluto at the time of birth. The planets represent the people, organisations, forces, cultures and emotions that make things happen in our world.

An astrological chart is 'read' by interpreting the positions of the planets in relationship to each other. The sun sign, ascendant and moon sign are the most vital to know. The houses represent the area of life where the signs are active and there are twelve, which are found in the cross-points of the chart. The star signs add information about the houses and the planets in them, and the aspects are the relationships between the planets which must be read together in order to form an holistic picture of the enquirer. Real astrology is complex and mathematical. It is unclear just how the early astrologers came to present such complex interpretations of all the planets and their influence on our lives, but anyone interested in the subject should go with an open mind, have a full chart reading and, of course, forget the newspaper variety!

Astrology is changing, especially as new planets have been discovered and people eagerly await the 'New Age' of Aquarius.

■ *What you can do*

Casting an astrological chart is complex and the interpretations are open to abuse. It may be easier to have your chart read by an experienced astrologer first before trying it yourself. The cost can be anywhere from £5 to £50, and good astrologers will ask for the date, place and exact time of birth in advance. You should be able to take home a fully prepared chart and a tape recording of the session where it is explained to you.

One of the most beneficial uses of astrology is in psychological astrology, which deals with the enquirer's personal relationships and perspective on life. It cannot offer the future on a plate but throws light and guidance on difficult periods or problems, including exploring crisis points in a person's life.

There are hundreds of books on astrology, including the do-it-yourself analysis types. Start perhaps by contacting the Astrological Association Book Service (see ADDRESSES TO CONTACT).

Workshops and organisations are arranged by the Astrological Association, the Astrological Lodge of London and The British Astrological and Psychic Society (see ADDRESSES TO CONTACT).

Aura

Every living person and creature is surrounded by a subtle energy field that we commonly call the aura. Most people cannot see someone else's aura but that doesn't mean that it isn't there. You can quite easily train yourself to 'see' this strange and often beautiful energy.

Some trained psychics and healers can see the human aura clearly enough to use it to make diagnoses of illnesses without even touching or speaking to the patient! Most psychics see the aura as something that is like a shimmering or gaseous light around the body, most often extending to between 10 and 30 centimetres from the skin.

For 5,000 years spiritual races, medical healers and all religions have spoken of a light that emanates from a person. Many spiritual teachings discuss the aura in detail. The Japanese Zen Buddhists, Native American Indians, Hindus in Indian writings, the Qabalah, even the Bible all refer to subtle energies surrounding the human body. Paintings of Jesus show him with a white light coming from his body; this is often more prominent around his head but it is always there in some form. Why did all the artists depict this? Someone, somewhere must have seen Jesus and his strong and clearly defined aura. It is said that a very advanced soul, a great spiritual leader or teacher, for example, will have a white and dazzling aura, showing how pure the person is inside. This might explain why people saw Jesus – and Buddha – with a pure white or golden aura. The Indian guru Sai Baba is said to have an aura that can be seen for hundreds of yards around his body.

In the past hundred years scientists have tried their best to capture the aura on film. One of the most famous experiments was that of the Russian scientist Semyon Kirlian, who invented Kirlian photography. His first experiment was by accident as he took a photograph of his own hand and passed a very high voltage of electricity through it. The resulting picture showed his hand, as he expected, but also white streams of energy radiating from it. Kirlian then spent the next 40 years 'proving' that everything that was alive was surrounded by what he called a 'biological plasma'. Kirlian's work has not been accepted by everyone, and even psychic supporters have questioned the basis of his electrical photography.

However slow science is at catching up with the human eye there seems to be no real dispute that auras exist. More and more people are opening their extrasensory perception (ESP) and 'seeing' the aura.

In reality the aura is not simply one block of colour surrounding the body. It is made up of several layers which have colours and textures of their own. You can 'see' only that part of the aura which you are ready to see, and few people have seen them all. Each layer looks different and has different functions for the body and soul. The layers are highly structured patterns of light which weave in colours and textures that are in constant motion. Some have a fluid-like texture, like the Milky Way, and they flow and move like gases. All the seven known layers move freely into each other. Each layer of the aura is associated with one of the chakras. (See CHAKRAS.)

In a normal, healthy person the seven layers of the aura may be visible, intact and clear. In an unhealthy person the aura may be fuzzy, have dark or blackened stains on it; it might be angry or even be trying to 'suck' energy from another person's aura. All experience will affect the aura, just as it will affect your physical body. If, for example, you have been working too hard over a number of years and drunk too much alcohol this will undoubtedly show on your face and inside your body in the form of illness, perhaps in your liver. The aura will also show these years of neglect, with stains around the liver area, and what has been described as a mucus-like fuzz around the auric layers. As reading the aura can be beneficial in medical diagnosis, it's a pity that many doctors refuse even to learn to see it, or to admit that it exists.

■ *What you can do*

Learn to see and feel the aura. Get a partner and put your hands some 20 centimetres apart at the back of the neck or head where the vibrations can be strong. Slowly draw your hands closer and further apart until you 'feel' the edge of the aura. You might sense heat or cold, gas or even a prickly energy when you get to the edge. This exercise is easy to do with one person sitting down and the other standing up behind them. You can put your hands all over the body of your partner, without ever touching them of course, just feeling the aura. Notice if the aura has a different texture around the legs or head. Notice if you can feel it more clearly after you have meditated.

Get your friend to sit on a chair with a plain background (white or a light colour is best), then sit about five metres away and look at the energy around your friend without looking directly at their body. Spend about ten minutes on this exercise if you can. Don't worry if you can't see anything for the first few times; practise whenever you can.

Most people manage at some point to see a haze, which often represents the first layer of the etheric body. Often this has a bluish tint, but you could well surprise yourself and see a multitude of colours or images.

Learn to protect your aura. Have you ever come away from someone feeling drained or confused, or have you been sucked into someone's problems without realising it? Do you always catch colds and flu? Is your aura open to abuse by other people?

One simple and effective way to start to protect yourself from other people's physical and emotional 'baggage' is to protect your aura. Imagine it as a force field around you that, if sufficiently strong and healthy, will be able to protect you and nurture you. Start each day with a simple affirmation, something like, 'My aura is strong and I am centred and happy within it.' This verbal support will help enormously, even if you do nothing else. You can also help by covering your aura in a shell, bandages, a balloon, in fact anything you can imagine that will effectively seal you from the pollution of the outside world. This way you can keep your energy in and avoid illness attacking your physical body from outside.

The most comprehensive, but complex, book on the human aura is *Hands of Light* by Barbara Ann Brennan (Bantam New Age Books, 1988). However, most books on the aura present the author's personal experience, and your experience may be different. Another book is *How to Read the Aura*, by W. E. Butler (Aquarian, 1979).

Look for auras around other living things, like trees, plants and flowers. The aura of an evergreen tree, for example, is very healing and calming and sitting against a tree for half an hour can revitalise you. Look for energy fields around objects like jewellery, doorknobs, etc. that people will have touched for a time.

See also HEALING, PSYCHOKINESIS, CHAKRAS, AFFIRMATIONS.

Automatic Writing

Automatic writing is a form of channelling where psychics can allow spirits to write through them. Recently a woman has claimed that Charles Dickens asked her to write a new novel for him, and this has already been published. You can find many similar works where the living author claims that their hand would move, unexplained, across the page writing out messages, lessons, even poetry.

Two French teenagers made automatic writing famous in 1804 when an intellectual spiritualist called Allan Kardec published their automatic writing in *The Spirits' Book*. Unfortunately for them, one of the reasons that it became so famous was because the girls were both thought to be very stupid. They preferred to go out to parties and talk about boys rather than anything else, so people were convinced that something else was operating through them when they sat down and scribbled out messages about profound things like ethereal and subtle matter!

In automatic writing you can receive messages either from those in the spirit world or from deep in your subconscious or your higher self.

■ *What you can do*

Sit in a semi-lit room with no interruptions. Get yourself into a state of deep relaxation or meditation, with your thought processes open to anything that comes along. Use a notebook and pen so that you can write effortlessly, and ask your mind to send you messages that can be read. Most people can sit for many sessions with nothing happening at all, but every now and then you might be inspired to write something meaningful. Some people who practise automatic writing say that their hands write so quickly across the page they are hardly able to read the scrawl but upon close scrutiny they find interesting and unpredictable information.

As well as automatic writing there have been many noted cases of automatic painting and drawing. One famous British healer, Matthew Manning, drew hundreds of tiny drawings and signatures from numerous artists when he was a teenager at school. These works have been published and authenticated from many sources as drawings done by artists other than Manning.

Always use protection for yourself if you practise automatic writing. Never allow beings to enter your space without permission, and be very clear about your purpose.

See CHANNELLING, PROTECTION, OUT-OF-BODY EXPERIENCES, HIGHER SELF.

Black Magic

The first citations and written accounts of priests misusing religious ceremonies to honour not God but the Devil took place well before the year AD 1000. Although the term 'black magic' was coined in the hysteria and aggressive times of the witch burnings of the fifteenth, sixteenth and seventeenth centuries, Christianity was moving fast into the lives of people in Europe, and the Mass was said to be a ritual embracing great power and energy from God. The more Christianity revered itself the more likely it was that someone was going to ridicule it and try to harness this 'power' for themselves. Stories abound, including those of priests who used the Christian sacraments of the body and blood of Christ to honour the Devil.

Women at this time were also being accused of practising black magic. Witches were often healers, ordinary women who were just thought to be too thin, short, ugly, clever or different for the time they were living in. While black magic did exist in some form it is unlikely that more than a handful of the estimated 10 million women and men who died over this period ever actually practised anything that could honestly be classed as evil.

The word 'black' probably came to be used in the context of black magic because of a primitive fear of the dark. Satan was also supposedly at his strongest in the dark night and many practitioners carried out their magic in darkness so as not to be seen by others.

Just like magic itself, black magic was carried out in order to change a situation, often for the pleasure and power that being in control of your life was supposed to bring. How you intend such magic to be used is the crucial issue: you can use your psychic energies for the benefit of others or to fuel your own desires and ego.

■ *What you can do*

Practising black magic is pathetic. Encouraging negative energy always rebounds on you and the people you practise it with, yet there are hundreds of books and films that continue to tell the story of people trying to harness power from the Devil to get back their youth, to live for ever or to get even with someone. I prefer real magic that only has beneficial side-effects! Don't use the term 'black' magic – say what you mean, be it anti-religious or egotistical power.

See MAGIC, EARTH MAGIC.

Breath

Breath: a strange thing to put in a book about spirituality, you could say, but our breath is one of the most empowering and important tools that we have for change. Breath is the spirit and stuff of life and many of us just don't realise that our breath can show us how we feel about ourselves and our spiritual connection to ourselves. For instance, imagine you've been hiding your real feelings or anger towards someone: you might notice that your breath is shallow, and that you will be breathing only from the top of your body, cutting off your real feelings and helping yourself to become semi-conscious. This type of breathing can become a bad habit and as a result our lives then become semi-conscious and we become semi-alive.

Breath is the most important tool used in meditation and using breathing effectively can help you get into a relaxed state where alpha waves are emitted, allowing you to work deeply on your subconscious and inner self (see also MEDITATION and DREAMS). It can help us to relax quickly and efficiently, slowing down the pulse and heart, bringing oxygen to all parts of the body and allowing visualisation techniques to be most effective.

■ *What you can do*

Start right now, by noticing your breath. Are you using your lungs to their full capacity? Are you energising and massaging all of your internal organs with your breath, or have you allowed fear, anger or similar emotions to stop your breath from working to support you?

Take a few deep breaths right now. Allow your body to be nurtured and enlivened by this.

Prepare a cleansing breath: breathe in through your nose slowly, allowing your chest to expand; feel the breath filling up your stomach and all your organs. As you breathe out, open your mouth: allow all the negativity, bad feelings and thoughts and worries of the day to escape through your mouth. Release tensions and fear as well as anger. Do this a few times, slowly and calmly.

If you get caught in a situation that you don't like, in an accident or argument for instance, use breath to help you. Powerful breaths can dispel your anger; deep breathing can recentre your body when you are nervous or you feel your legs are shaky or your stomach is in knots.

Buddhism

The Indian prince of the Saka clan, Gautama Siddhartha, lived in Nepal about 500 years BC and was thought to be the originator of Buddhist ideas. Myths and legends indicate that the prince was not altogether happy with his life and one day, outside the safety of his palace, he saw horrific suffering in the form of an old man, a sick man, a dead man and a holy man. This led him to believe in the pursuit of happiness through spiritual enlightenment, understanding that life moves all the time (as symbolised by the old man), that suffering exists (symbolised by the sick man), that death is inevitable (symbolised by the dead man), and that each one of us is searching for spiritual enlightenment (symbolised by the holy man).

After toying with how to find such enlightenment, Siddhartha sat underneath a bodhi tree and discovered knowledge of all past memories, all present energies and the ever-moving chain of cause and effect, known as karma. This knowledge meant that he was then called Shakyamuni Buddha, which means 'enlightened one'. He then spent the rest of his life teaching and sharing his knowledge with others, concentrating on the evaporation of suffering which is central to Buddhist philosophy. The principle teachings are called the Four Noble Truths and the Eightfold Path.

The Four Noble Truths:

1. There is no existence without suffering – *Dukkha*.
2. The cause of suffering is personal/egotistical desire – *Samudaya*.
3. The state of elimination of desire – *Nirodha*.
4. The way to eliminate such desire is the Noble Eightfold Path – *Magga*.

The Noble Eightfold Path of spiritual development leading to enlightenment:

1. Right view
2. Right mental attitude or motive
3. Right speech
4. Right action
5. Right pursuits
6. Right effort
7. Right mindfulness
8. Right contemplation

Collectively, these teachings of the Buddha are known as the Dharma. The Buddhist philosophy is that enlightenment will be achieved when desire and suffering are extinct.

After the death of Shakyamuni Buddha his teachings and ideas spread through the East to Sri Lanka, Burma and Thailand and to Tibet, China and Japan. Two slightly varying schools of Buddhism arose in the following 300 years as the ideas of the religion spread out across the world. The main difference between the two schools is that the Theravada school believes that enlightenment is not possible in one lifetime, even by a monk. The Mahayana school believes that buddhahood, or enlightenment, can be achieved in this lifetime and that everyone has the potential for such enlightenment.

The Lotus Sutra, written about AD 220 in north-west India is from the Mahayana school of Buddhism and is the scripture most closely associated with the true intentions of Shakyamuni.

In the thirteenth century, Nichiren Daishonin, a priest of the Tendai sect who studied the scriptures of many religions including Zen came to the conclusion that 'Buddhism equals daily life'. He believed that the original message of Buddhism had become lost over the past 1000 years. In Japan he practised Buddhism which directly criticised the Japanese authorities, so was exiled in 1261. An attempt was made to execute him which, the story goes, was stopped when lightning struck and blinded his executioner.

Smaller sects of Buddhism have since appeared all over the world and many people have been persecuted for practising the faith. Even today the people of Tibet have been killed or exiled for practising Tibetan Buddhism, and the Dalai Lama, head of the spiritual Buddhist centre of Tibet, has been exiled by the Chinese authorities for many years.

The spiritual quest of Buddhism is close to that of many New Age ideas, and since Buddhism came to Britain in the 1920s, access and groups have been spreading. Many people include Buddhist ideas within their own spiritual path.

■ *What you can do*

Contact the Buddhist Society, which has details of Buddhist groups and schools in your area (see ADDRESSES TO CONTACT).

Learn Buddhist meditation, essentially sitting, doing nothing, and then focusing on the breath. See BREATH, MEDITATION.

Read *What the Buddha Taught*, by Walpola Rahula (Wisdom Press, 1990); *The World of Buddhism*, by H. Bechert and E. Gombrich (Thames & Hudson, 1980); and *The Buddhist Handbook*, by John Snelling (Rider Books, 1992).

Candles

Candles are used in spiritual, psychic and healing work and it is said that they invoke the presence of spirit in your work. Candles present an atmosphere just as oils, herbs and incense can. They are used in meditation for reflection, in prayer and in magic work to provide a focus.

■ *What you can do*

Whenever you hear of someone who is ill, or going through bad times, or even celebrating, light a candle for them, sending a message of light and healing energy their way.

Light candles for friends and family, for situations that you are worried about. Choose the colour by what feels right for you and link this colour up with the chakra colours and the colours of the energy you wish to evoke. The more you make your candle-lighting into a ritual the more potent the magic will be. When you blow out a candle send the energy of the light towards someone. Whisper the name of the person that you have dedicated the light to and it will get to them. Like absent healing, the light will reach them and be absorbed as goodness wherever it is needed.

Chakras

The body has a noticeable set of energy centres, known as the chakras. They can also be called the psychic centres and they have been seen and mentioned in spiritual texts, magical works and ancient religious scriptures for thousands of years. They are known to be a critical factor in psychic work, drawing on energy from the universe to heal people, and even channelling the spirits from the other worlds.

Each chakra relates to one of the glands in our body, and to our nervous system. Our glands are linked with each other and the balance of our physical bodies is directly connected to the well-being and balance of our chakras.

The word 'chakra' comes from the *rishis* (Indian holy men or seers). Its meaning is wheels, as the inside of the chakra energy seems to whirl like a Catherine wheel: energy light radiates in spokes pointing outwards from the centre. The Chinese call chakras the *dantian*, and know them as the centres that allow energy to flow back and forth. Many people have described them as bell-shaped flowers that have thin tentacles moving outwards which pick up energy and use or store it. The stems are joined to a channel which runs parallel to the spine and links them all together, passing information from one chakra point to another and refining the energy as it travels upwards towards the head.

There are different names and varying numbers of chakras but the most commonly agreed figure is seven main points with several others of lesser importance.

The first chakra is situated at the base of the spine and is called the *base chakra*. It connects us with our will to live, our survival and our energy. It is usually associated with the colour red and the adrenal glands. It is the chakra that 'grounds' us in physical reality and if it should be damaged, say by a fall, or blocked, it will cause a draining of energy from the whole body.

To increase the flow of energy into your body you can simply sense or imagine energy pouring into this point and running up your spine. Your body will only take what it needs from this exercise. People who are in control of and have an energised base chakra are bursting with vitality and energy and can often heal and offer energy to others around them.

The second main chakra, known as the *sacral chakra*, is related to the endocrine glands, which are concerned with reproduction and sexual activity, and with corresponding glands. It sits just below the navel and absorbs vital energy for the body. It is also concerned with basic human emotions and physical creativity. The colour orange is usually associated with the sacral chakra.

The *solar plexus chakra* is concerned with emotions and intellect and the powers of the mind. It is the place where our social awareness comes from and is a psychic centre because it is connected to the astral world. In your body, the solar plexus is situated just below the breast-bone and is related to the stomach, the small intestine and the pancreas. It relates mainly to the colour yellow, and is responsible for clear thinking, studying and decision-making.

The *heart chakra*, coloured green, is the beginning of compassion and sympathy, how to love and care for another person or persons. It is situated in the centre of your chest and is related directly to the thymus gland and the lungs and heart. It creates a balance between body, mind and spirit.

The *throat chakra*, situated at the centre of the throat, is the centrepoint for spiritual will relating to the thyroid and organs of the upper chest, such as the bronchi, and is of course related to the voice. It is the colour blue and concerns all forms of communication and creative expression. People who can speak many foreign languages often have a very mature throat chakra.

The *brow chakra*, is situated at the place of the third eye and is associated with spiritual will, vision, intuition and unseen perception. It is related to the pituitary gland and is coloured indigo. (See THIRD EYE.)

The final of the seven main chakras is the *crown chakra*, which usually means the association with the Godhead, or universe. It is related to the pineal gland and the colour violet. The crown chakra and the brow chakra work closely together and are said to be our connection to the spiritual world, and our spiritual will to be. We can gain self-awareness, calmness and peace from this chakra.

The chakras are also connected to the aura, and the aura protects the chakras from damage whenever it can. After psychic work you must clearly and specifically close down your aura, or protect it in order to protect yourself from unwanted entry into your psychic space (see PROTECTION) and to prevent long-term damage to your chakras.

■ *What you can do*

Meditate and imagine that you can feel or see your chakras. Use colour or the physical location of the chakra to sense them. Can you feel any different vibrations as you move up your body towards your crown chakra?

If you feel you need healing in a certain area then match the colour with the chakras and use in meditation through visualisation, in food (e.g. eating vegetables of this colour), burning appropriate candles and so on to help you. An appropriate visualisation and meditation is as follows.

Sit comfortably with your back straight. Visualise each of the seven chakra colours coming into your body one at a time as you breathe, starting with red. Breathe the colour in through your left foot and up towards your crown chakra (just above the head) and then down the other side of your body and out of your right foot. After each colour you can then surround yourself in all seven colours at once, energising your aura. Relax and meditate for as long as necessary.

Many books have explanations of the chakras. Those that are worth reading include *Spiritual Healing: Energy Medicine for Today*, by Jack Angelo (Element, 1991), and *Journey through the Chakras: Exercises for Healing and Internal Balancing*, by Klahsbernd Vollmar (Gateway Books, 1987).

See also HEALING, AURA, MEDIUMS, MEDITATION.

Channelling

When a soul 'dies' in the physical world it has many choices about its future. The soul can decide to come back again in another body (see REINCARNATION), or it can decide to learn from its mistakes or experiences by observing or listening to others both in the spirit world or on earth, or even on another planet, should it wish. Some could decide to talk to humans through people whom we call mediums or channels. These people allow the spirit to use their body, sometimes for hours at a time; through this the spirit can talk and have a conversation with anyone. Channels have been known for thousands of years and there are many famous cases.

While in public the authorities would have us believe that no one can speak to or communicate with someone who is dead, in reality they must know that it happens all the time. In Colin Wilson's book *Beyond the Occult*, the American researcher Professor James Hyslop summed up many people's feelings about the evidence and proof of such meetings: 'I regard the existence of discarnate spirits as scientifically proved and I no longer refer to the sceptic as having any right to speak on the subject. Any man who does not accept the existence of discarnate spirits and the proof of it is either ignorant or a moral coward. I give him short shrift, and do not propose to argue with him on the subject.'

We can often learn much from those spirits who have died and decide to come back and tell us things about 'the other side'. However, be warned! Just because a spirit is dead it doesn't necessarily follow that it is clever or wise. Someone who was unwise during their physical life here may not have learnt much just because they have died.

Without exception, one thing the channels all tell us is that life after death exists. Some people who were non-believers during their lives here spend a lot of energy trying to get through to us now to tell us this. You can meet a channel, hear teaching or ask questions about personal things by looking for a reputable group in places such as the School of Channelling, the College of Psychic Studies or through your local Spiritualist church.

When a human 'channels' someone from the spirit world they must let go of their own ego completely in order to allow the spirit in. Many people find this very difficult and the result can be a mixed message, often garbled or unclear. One of the most noted psychics this century, Alice Bailey, suggests that many channels find that they are not channelling another spirit at all but speaking through their higher selves. As your higher self has many wise answers to questions this is not entirely a bad thing, although it is different from another entity sharing your body.

■ *What you can do*

Don't play around with channelling. Powerful and strange energies can enter your body without you even knowing, if you open up to them. Far better to learn the safety techniques outlined and go to classes and workshops.

If you meet a spirit that has entered another body you can quite simply ask if they are friendly, or come in peace. If you feel unsure or nervous show them the universal peace symbol of a cross in a circle, which represents balance and protection, and ask them three times if they come in peace. This usually helps to get rid of any undesirable forces.

Safety in channelling

1. Meditate and prepare yourself, including 'earthing' yourself by making sure your feet are on the ground and that you are connected, through your imagination, to the earth.
2. Ask your guides to protect you and never allow yourself to be used by undesirable forces or spirits.
3. Protect the room/area that you are working in with a 'light, white safety bubble' by simply imagining it, and always visualise it before you begin.
4. Don't do it on your own, and only get experienced people to sit with you, creating an energy field. They should be people you can trust to help you and psychically protect you.
5. Ask that only good light come towards you, and it will.
6. Be prepared to meet yourself.
7. Ask specific and detailed questions about the spirit you have met that will help you to identify them.

You will recognise a real soul by noting the following:

1. A wise spirit never tells you what to do, always offers loving advice.
2. A wise spirit never tells you what will happen in the future; it can only offer various scenarios of what the future might hold for you but reminds you that you have a free will and that you are in control of your destiny.

3. A wise spirit will offer insight to you that will make you grow and learn.

Read *Soul to Soul* and *Spirit Speaks*, magazines of channelled information and teachings (see MAGAZINES).

Books on channelling include *Seth Speaks*, by Jane Robert (Bantam Books, 1974); *Gildas Communicates*, by Ruth White and Mary Swainson (C. W. Daniel, 1971); *Spiritual Realisation: Inner Values in Everyday Life/Chan*, by Ivy Northage (Pilgrim Books, 1987); and *The Guide Book: Where There is Love, HA On Life & Living: A Channelled Teaching of Our Time*, by Tony Neate (Pegasus Foundation, 1992).

See MEDIUMS, MEDITATION, SPIRITUALISM.

Chanting

Chanting is used by many religions and spiritual groups as an ancient way to communicate with the universe through the energy of sound. Buddhist and yogic chanting is similar to chanting rituals used today in Europe by meditation groups in the New Age movement. Native American and other tribal peoples also use chanting in their spiritual work.

Essentially chanting works because it changes the physical body, bringing in more oxygen, which has a powerful effect on the human brain. It changes the mind by inducing a trance-like state which is relaxing, and thus enhances the chance of spiritual or mystical experiences. It feeds the chakras and the aura which offer a heightened sensitivity to energies around the person.

Sound makes a vibration. The whole body vibrates, even the inner organs, the aura and the chakra. Chanting brings better life force, equalling better balance and health.

Taize chanting techniques use Latin verse and rounds together with quiet spiritual reflection to create a very special technique used in Christian centres around Europe.

■ What you can do

Buddhist centres are probably the best places to learn chanting for yourself but you can see chanting in evidence in all religions and festivals.

Good bookshops sell tape cassettes of chanting, including those of the teach-yourself variety. Look for Leo Rutherford's selection. There is also the Prana, an ethnic chanting group who organise an annual summer group (See ADDRESSES TO CONTACT).

Clairvoyance

Clairvoyance simply means the ability to see clearly. In its wider context it means the ability to see by paranormal means, like seeing energies that others cannot, ghosts, spirits or other life forms not directly connected to humans.

Information obtained through clairvoyance is often very hard to prove unless many people claim to have 'seen' the same thing at the same time. Even then stories can be muddled, which puts doubt in our minds. Ask three people to look at a flowerpot and then describe what they can see and you will get some idea of how difficult it is to get people to describe the same thing. Then try and do this for something that people can barely see and you will understand how difficult it is!

Most people who have clairvoyant experiences find that they have to be in a very relaxed state; often they are meditating or on the edge of sleep and wakefulness when they have their first clairvoyant experience. The brain must be relaxed and calm. It could be that what we see is the product of our subconscious mind, and for many people who claim to have had clairvoyant experiences this is probably the most likely explanation. It is certainly possible to want to see something so much that you can use your imagination to convince yourself that it is in front of you. But for many people clairvoyant experiences have become a way of life and even the most sceptical scientific minds have been unable to explain just how these people can see clearly something that happened before they were born, or something that happens in the future. Most clairvoyants can 'see' the pictures in an unusual way, which distinguishes them from imagination: they are often in 3D, for instance. Once you have had a real clairvoyant experience it will be unmistakable for you.

One famous case retold in Colin Wilson's *Beyond the Occult* is that of Eileen Garrett who was told, in advance of the events, of the deaths of successive aunts, uncles, husbands, children and other relatives. She would often see a vision of the person coming towards her telling her of their death, like a warning. At first her very strict aunt, with whom she lived in Ireland, did not believe her and would beat her for telling such stories, even when they came true within a few days! Eventually Eileen grew up and travelled to America, where she carried out experiments proving her clairvoyant abilities with serious researchers and professors. She soon came to be accepted as a very gifted psychic as she was able to see and talk as a medium with various people who had died many years before. (See MEDIUMS and CHANNELLING.)

People who see auras and energies around bodies are also described as clairvoyant (see AURAS). The energy fields which are around all our bodies are usually invisible but gifted clairvoyants can train themselves to see this energy, even sometimes to see it in colours.

Tony Neate, one of the counsellors at the College of Psychic Studies in London runs weekend workshops on psychic awareness. He says that when he started work nearly forty years ago there were very few people who saw auras or similar energies, but in the 1990s nearly 95 per cent of those on his courses are able to 'see' or feel something clairvoyantly. This, he claims, is further proof of a New Age in which more people are beginning to awaken different parts of themselves and their psychic abilities.

■ *What you can do*

If you think you have had a clairvoyant experience yourself you will probably be just like most people, and there isn't very much you can do about it! If you want to train yourself, contact a reputable place like the College of Psychic Studies or Runnings Park Centre for Healing (see ADDRESSES TO CONTACT). The more work you do on yourself with personal growth and meditation the more likely you are to have a clairvoyant experience.

See THIRD EYE, TELEPATHY, ASTRAL PLANE, GHOSTS, CHANNELLING, DÉJÀ VU, MEDIUMS, PARAPSYCHOLOGY, PSYCHIC, PROTECTION.

Crystals and Precious Stones

Women and men have worn precious and semiprecious stones and crystals for centuries but it is only in recent years that the New Age has relearned a deeper and more significant reason for their beauty. They are all capable of transmitting subtle energies that, in conjunction with our knowledge of spiritual healing and psychic energies, can be used to heal, to protect, to energise and radiate love.

Crystals and stones have been used in magic and ceremonies as amulets (see AMULETS) and as gifts of great power. It is no accident that stones, crystals and diamonds are given to others as a sign of love and respect, and worn as a sign of power.

Crystals are of special importance as they represent the force of water, earth, air and fire. Quartz crystals, which are said to have taken over 10,000 years to form, are petrified water, known as silicon dioxide. As the water petrifies within the earth it brings together sand and oxygen and magically transforms the water into a hardened, glass-like crystal. According to Diane Stein, the feminist spiritual writer of *The Women's Spirituality Book*, a quartz crystal absorbs both magnetism from the earth's core and radiation from the sun and emits that energy. The energy can attract itself to the human aura, and this is where its special abilities take effect. In conjunction with meditation and psychic healing they can be used as powerful tools, like a magic wand.

Many of the stones and crystals available today have differing qualities. Like any products from the earth, caution should be used in their collection, use and availability. Some of the most beautiful gemstones have been mined from the very Amazon rainforest that has been of so much concern because of threats to ecological and biological diversity.

Main crystals and their current uses

Amethyst. A beautiful spiritual stone to use for meditation and helping aid restful sleep. It is associated with the crown chakra and is usually deep violet in colour. It is a very grounding and clarity-giving stone.

Rose quartz. The most commonly found crystal available, this is used for healing and for love. It connects with the heart chakra and is good to cure heartache and to release pent-up emotions. It is a gentle, loving crystal that is not dangerous to use. Also good for healing kidneys.

Clear quartz. True clear quartz is all-purpose and all-healing, as it connects with all the colours and energies in the chakras. It can cure headaches if you put a crystal close to your pillow and it can help you through periods of stress, such as examinations. Quartz crystal with lines of colour, or rutilant quartz, will amplify your work.

Emerald. A green stone, which works with the heart chakra and invokes psychic energy. It is said to have divination properties. Emerald is a harmonising stone and should not be mixed in jewellery with other stones.

Garnet. A red/brown stone that has sexual energy all around it. It is associated with the root chakra and the blood in our bodies. Anyone with energy, circulation or blood problems should be helped by wearing this.

Red jasper. An energetic stone that works through the sacral and solar plexus. It is harmonising and earthy and keeps both the body and the mind hot! It is apparently good for liver problems.

Topaz. A strong yellow crystal that clears disease and stress like headaches. It works through the solar plexus and is good for the kidneys and the transition between life and death.

Opal. The family of opal gems serve a great spiritual task. You can find all colours of the chakra in opal, but the black is said to be the most highly developed and can work on all spiritual and physical centres at the same time. It is also called the 'stone of the spirits'.

Jade. Often called 'the prince of peace and tranquillity', jade is an important and useful stone to hold. It will never harm anyone who wears it and it clears negativity and depression. It is associated with deep inner and natural beauty and is a tranquil shade of green.

Diamond. This is the most clear and expensive of all the gems, being made for the highest of all possible spiritual work.

Many people are unaware of the potency stored up inside a diamond, which gives energy, courage, long life and wealth. Wearing a diamond and thinking negatively will warp and twist its magic. Combine a diamond with any other gem and you automatically enhance its power.

■ *What you can do*

When you buy crystals and gemstones always perform a ritual cleansing with salt water to clear the energies of whoever has touched them. Don't buy stones that are too big to hold in your hand, and quartz in particular only needs to be shaped at one end to be effective.

For more information read *The Women's Spirituality Book*, by Diane Stein (Llewellyn, 1986); and *Good Magic*, by Marina Medici (Prentice-Hall, 1988). For a spiritual/esoteric perspective try *Healing Stones*, by Julia Lorusso and Joel Glick (Brotherhood of Life, 1976).

See CHAKRAS, RITUALS, MAGIC.

Death

All of us will die at some time or another whether we like it or not. What frightens us about death is usually the fact that in our society no one talks about it except in an emotional, negative and sad way. Of course it is sad and painful when a good friend, parent, sister or brother dies, but if you are more aware of what happens to that person after they have stopped breathing it can sometimes help the pain to ease a little more quickly. Our society has stopped us from seeing, talking about and learning about death. Our culture has removed us from the land and nature, including seasons which connect us to natural events, for example animals dying. Our culture forgets to celebrate life when death occurs.

A common story of what happens after death is this one from a young woman from Surrey who died in 1992. As this woman was clairvoyant she came back to tell her clairvoyant friends what happened to her after she stopped breathing.

First of all she was aware that people were talking about her and she was watching them, and her body. She was floating in the room that she died in. Then she clearly remembers seeing a magnificent light in a sort of tunnel. She started to go up the tunnel and at the end of this tunnel she was met by her mother and another woman. Her mother had died several years before this. At the end of the tunnel she was greeted by a small group of people whom she recognised as her guides, those spirits who had been helping her throughout her waking life. They all shook hands excitedly and celebrated her arrival. She felt very happy, even overjoyed, as if she had come home. Then they all disappeared very quickly and she is convinced that she will never see them again. Even so, she felt very happy about this. She was then taken to a special sort of hospital in Spiritland where she was laid on a bed in order to recover. After a while this woman, who was never very good at lying still when she was alive, decided to get up and take a look around. To her astonishment she found that she could not walk, but she glided along! She then went to see her family, who were obviously upset and were crying about her death. She attended her own funeral and saw and heard everyone, and she 'visited' many friends and relatives. Of course only a few who could already 'see' spirits were able to recognise her. However, many people who have had close friends die say that they can sense or feel someone around them watching and listening.

Often our friends come back to us in our dreams, allowing us to say goodbye or settle some disagreement or discussion so that both parties feel complete. Our dreams are just as valid as our waking life in this respect and you can be sure that if you dream of the person who has died they are likely to be trying to contact you, often to say that everything is all right. (See DREAMS.)

The following can help if someone close to you dies:

1. Don't despair. They have moved on to another part of their existence and you will see them again in time. Don't deny your feelings, if you are angry, or feeling let down, for instance. Find a good and wise friend who will listen, and tell them everything you can.
2. Light candles, pray, talk to them. They can hear you, and giving them positive energy helps them to recover as well as you. It is a form of healing in itself, for both of you.
3. Forgive yourself. If you have had a row with them, for instance, do forgive yourself. No one dies because of someone else and in death that person can often see other points of view that they may not have while they were alive.
4. Forgive them, whatever they have done.

5. Notice your dreams and your feelings. Be comforted that if you sense that person close to you when you are in despair, they probably are there, right beside you. Often they try and comfort you even though you cannot see them. If you believe it you are more likely to see them too.

How to prepare for your own death:

1. Accept that you will, at some point, die. The time and how you die is one of life's eternal mysteries. Is the way you act just now the way you like to be remembered? Are you as loving, compassionate and supportive as you want to be? Have you really done what you want to do in life, have you followed your passion rather than what you think others say you should do? These are questions that you will ask yourself continuously throughout your life. Don't leave it until you are 90 to ask them, start now and you might find that living can be exciting and fulfilling once you let go of the fear of death. Give your life meaning.
2. Meditate. (See MEDITATION.) Choose which form of meditation is best for you and prepare yourself for another life after the one you have had. Some people are told in advance that they are dying, perhaps when they have some types of cancer or other fatal illness.
3. You could use this opportunity to prepare yourself fully to live in the present and be ready to move onwards; don't just wait to die, live first. Don't abuse your body: valuing life is important and the way you value your physical body can make a marked difference to your attitude to life and death.
4. Be conscious and aware of your body in life and you will be able to feel and see death when it comes. Understanding reincarnation, for instance, will give you a good perspective when you die. You are less likely to get stuck on the earth or the astral plane as a ghost if you are aware that it is possible to move on to the other side. Don't escape through suicide, planetary despair, lack of values. Hold positive life models: your future is part of a greater whole, within yourself and the universe.

People often fear dying in pain from awful illnesses, but today's medical advances have helped people to die painlessly but consciously. Counselling and special facilities have also become the norm, and hospices are places where people can die with loving support and dignity.

The actual act of dying is not painful in itself: you simply breathe out and then you don't breathe in again. Most of the pain people feel is from illness, fear of death itself and what lies beyond it. One important thing to remember is that there are no judgements except your own; this means that if you think there is a hell after death and that you should go to it you probably will. If, on the other hand, you believe that after death you will be in heaven, you probably will be. Whatever happens, there will be a time when you reflect on what you have done, when you will watch and analyse your life and what happened in it. Many spirits say that this is a very painful process for many people, and it could be near to what we think of as hell. We simply cannot ignore the actions we have taken in our lives, they will have affected others and we have to be aware and learn from them. In all, it is a good process, moving us forward all the time, allowing us to learn and grow.

See REINCARNATION, MEDITATION, GUARDIAN ANGELS OR GUIDES.

Films to see: *Ghost*, staring Whoopi Goldberg; *Truly, Madly, Deeply* (Juliet Stevenson and Alan Rickman); *It's a Wonderful Life* (James Stewart).

Get counselling on death and bereavement. Don't be embarrassed about your pain. Be prepared to contact counsellors and healers to help you if someone close to you dies.

Read *The Tibetan Book of the Dead*, translated by Francesca Fremantle and Chogyam Trungpa (Shambhala Dragon Editions, 1987) for a Buddhist perspective; and Alice Walker's *To Hell with Dying* (Hodder & Stoughton, 1991).

Déjà Vu

The word comes from the French 'already seen' and there are many opinions on the meaning of the strange moment in our lives when we just know that we have been in that particular situation before. For just a split second our minds might forget and then switch back on again like a computer but it has lost a vital moment of memory and therefore believes that the moment before was past memory. Another version is that our subconscious creates a memory of something that happened before and tries to link it with this new situation, confusing the mind.

Another version is that time, which according to new metaphysics (the science of thought) exists only on a physical plane, is like a length of rope which we can run along to see ourselves in the past and in the future whenever we want and that we sometimes do this unconsciously thus producing *déjà vu*.

■ *What you can do*

Notice when you have a *déjà vu* experience. Are you tired? Emotional? Spiritual? Excited? Make a note and carry out your own research. Read *Time* by Marie-Louise von Franz, Thames and Hudson (1978) and *Living Magically* by Gill Edwards, Piatkus books (1991).

Divination

Divination is the art of those who see the future or, more simply, fortune-telling. Over the centuries, cultures and societies have sought answers to their questions and worries about what the future holds for them. From ancient shamanistic trances and spirit summonings to modern tea-leaf readings, people have called upon supernatural forces to aid them in their lives.

We would all like to be lucky, and to know that luck may be just around the corner would keep anyone happy, even if only for a short while. This may be the modern basis for using cards and the stars to tell us the future. But it seems that humans have always wanted to ask a power higher than themselves for help with their plans and dreams, whether trivial or important. Consultation with soothsayers or fortune-tellers may not give you the answers you were looking for but they will often give you something to think about that perhaps you were unprepared for or have been resisting for a while.

A type of divination called 'ecstatic' or 'intuitive' was widely used by ancient civilisations. This form of futuristic knowledge was obtained by shamans who would go into a trance and talk to spirits. Such people were revered all over the globe for their special abilities to use meditation and trance to see the other worlds. (See CHANNELLING.)

Tarot cards and rune stones are just two of the many hundreds of methods of 'inductive' divination using objects. Rune stones are thought to have been used first as long ago as 10,000 BC, and they have remained almost the same during all that time.

However, divination isn't just about knowing what is in your stars for today. In ancient times it held much more spiritual significance for a community that had very little information from other sources. Rituals, ceremonies, stories, dreams, teachings, trances, meditations, and weather forecasts all helped communities, and their collective consciousness and understanding of each other and natural events.

■ *What you can do*

See what methods of divination your family and friends already recognise and use. Are they held in high regard or ridiculed? Have any of them been handed down from generation to generation? Why do you think people still need to look at their sun stars every day in the newspaper?

Read the best historical book on divination available: *The World Atlas of Divination*, edited by John Matthews (Eddison Sadd, 1992). See ASTROLOGY, RUNES, I CHING, TAROT CARDS, DOWSING, DREAMS, SHAMANISM and NUMEROLOGY for a more indepth look at some of the various forms of divination used today.

Dowsing

The ancient art of dowsing began with the need to find a basic necessity – water. Hazel or willow twigs were cut into the letter 'Y' and then used to dowse for water under the ground. When moved over water, the twig would twitch and jump if water was directly underneath. For this to happen the wood itself must be sufficiently flexible and you must put some care into choosing and cutting the piece, although for modern dowsing many woods will do if you can't find hazel.

A typical dowsing rod is about a metre long, including the fork and about 2 or 3 centimetres in diameter. When holding a dowsing rod you should have your hands turned upwards with your thumbs at the ends of the twig. Apply some pressure on the twig until there seems to be an element of tension between the forks which you are holding with each hand. You will now realise why you need supple twigs!

Start to walk at a steady pace around a piece of land, say your local park or school grounds. The tension in your hands and in the dowsing rod will move when it can locate the energy of water. Start with the rod pointing slightly upwards so that when you hit an underground water source you can feel it changing and going downwards.

You can source anything from a well to a modern-day pipe that brings water to your house. Underground streams are evident but be sure to mark the point from each side of the stream to determine the centre point of the water and direction of the flow. Dowsing for water isn't really magic, any more than using a compass is, and with a little practice about 80 per cent of people should be able to get some response. Dowsing really became accepted by the scientific community after the amazing findings of a physicist and special adviser to the United States Army, Professor Harvalik. His experiments in the late 1960s basically proved that water gives off a charge, like an electrical charge and that almost anyone can find it, provided they are tuned in to it. Professor Harvalik also proved that if you drank half a pint of water before you started you could increase the likelihood of a good result! His conclusion was that the human body, made up of 70 per cent water, acts like a magnet and when it has a pliable tool, like a dowsing rod, it can detect the water so vital for the survival of our species.

One important part of Professor Harvalik's studies was that the dowser could also 'tune in' to anything he or she wanted, like metals, food or lost objects. For this to be really effective you should use a pendulum (see PENDULUM POWER).

■ *What you can do*

Read *Water Divining* by Ralph Whitlock (David & Charles, 1982) and *Pendulum Dowsing*, by Tom Graves (Element, 1989) for a good all-round history and account of how to dowse for water and similar energies.

Make your own dowsing rod and see what happens. Try to use it at different times, especially over areas you know to have water. Does the energy change at night? In the full moon? When you forget to concentrate or only when you think hard about finding it? Look for native Aboriginal stories from Australia about people who could smell water without using a dowsing rod.

Dreams

Every person, in every society, has dreamed at one stage or another in their lives. There is no one that will tell you that dreams do not exist and yet there is no proof whatsoever that they do. We believe that they exist because so many of us have them. Artists and poets, writers and thinkers have pondered and shown us their dreams over many centuries, but all interpretations and explanations are limited and personal.

In ancient cultures dreams were revered as important messages from the gods and goddesses. In the Bible dreams were often a sign of a great happening, foretelling disasters or wonders.

Today, thanks mainly to the work of Sigmund Freud and Carl Jung, dreams have taken on a much more personal and individual message, but they are the very essence of our communication with our inner God or higher self and our unconscious mind and the other worlds.

Although Freud was instrumental in getting us to change our thoughts about dreams he nearly always linked his patients' dreams with their previous experiences or early sexual activity, which was rather limiting. Even Jung, who disagreed with Freud's ideas after a time, was limited in his view of the way that dreams could be expanded and interpreted.

There are of course many types of dreams. Here are a few.

Lucid dreams

In these you actually feel and know that the dream is taking place while you are dreaming it but the dream continues, even so. You can alter lucid dreams at will: for example if you are running to catch a bus you can make the bus stop so that you can get on it. Lucid dreams are very good omens, especially if you are having a bad dream as you can decide to change the ending or wake up. The Senoi tribal peoples always taught their children at a very early age to practise lucid dreaming. This is especially good if you seem to be having a recurring dream or nightmare. You can decide that the next time you dream this way you will solve the problem and you will probably find that you never have the dream again.

Recurring dreams

Dreams that you have night after night must be looked at. According to current interpretations and, indeed, common sense, the dream is trying to tell you something about yourself. The interpretation must be yours, however. If a red rose means love to you then it probably will do in your dream but if you think hard and find that a red rose means danger, then that is likely to be what it means for you. The higher self and subconscious mind often have only a number of ways of communicating with you, especially if you haven't developed other methods of hearing. Dreams are one way that your subconscious can tell you what's going on. Recurring dreams indicate a more serious and almost insistent message. Follow the examples of how to record and interpret your dreams listed at the end of this section and see what happens.

Prophetic dreams

A few dreams are really prophetic. Often they are warnings of future events like deaths and accidents. Sometimes a warning dream might shake you so hard that you change your mind in a certain way so that you don't attract the event towards you. Other times you will be powerless to do anything. Many dreams are of aeroplane crashes, major disasters and accidents but never have enough detail for it to mean anything significant until after the event.

Nightmares

Frightening dreams and nightmares can have a variety of sources. It may be possible that eating certain foods late at night does bring on scary-monster-type experiences. People say that cheese and chocolate late at night can do this, as well as watching horror movies. The truth is that you may well be influenced by what's in your stomach; stomach acids may induce responses in your brain that activate or speed up the 'hairy-scary' kind of dream.

Nightmares can also be condensed messages about things that aren't going too well in your life. If you have a nightmare that you are being chased to the point of near death you could look at the commitments you have that may be wearing you out, or the fears you have picked up from others around you.

Replay dreams

Sometimes you dream that you are doing exactly the same thing as you did during the day, replaying each moment, but often with a little twist of difference here and there, just enough to let you know that it is a dream. These dreams are said to be the mind working over and storing the information it has collected during the day and the day's activities in as much detail as possible. Often you may not have liked a particular event or something you said, and that part of your dream may have been changed to see what could have happened. This type of dream is very useful for sorting things out.

Material dreams

Your dream suddenly encompasses a loud telephone ringing. As you drift back into consciousness you realise that the telephone wasn't in your dream at all – the telephone really was ringing, and you jump up to answer it! Material dreams often include real-life events that cross the divide between your waking and your sleeping reality.

Spirit dreams

Many people have had wonderful dreams in which they have met friends in the spirit world who have previously died.

Sometimes a good dream like this can heal past relationships, make up for lost moments and quarrels and settle things between people so that they can both move on to their own future, whether dead or alive. A woman in California divorced her husband with much acrimony and years later they were still not talking. Only three years after he had died did she meet him again in a wonderful dream where they had a picnic and told each other everything that had happened to them both in the period when they hadn't spoken. At the end of the meal they parted the best of friends and she claims to have felt an inner peace about herself and the relationship ever since. A healing had taken place either in her own subconscious mind or with him in the spirit world; either way it was an important healing for them both. Other spirit dreams include being given messages, meeting guides and discussing futures and problems.

Hypnagogic dreams

These are sleep-inducing dreams. Not as clear or deep as dreams in the later stages of sleep, they often 'sort out the day' for us, showing us isolated images and pictures that make no real sense, rather like replay dreams. This type of dream is most often found to have occurred in the first one and a half hours of sleep.

Why do we dream and how?

Scientists have been able to monitor brain activity and how our bodies react to internal stimuli. It seems that we dream in order to keep our emotional and mental mind in balance. Our dreams come from a vast mixture of experiences and thoughts, meetings with others and visits to the future.

Keep a dream diary. If you have a problem remembering your dreams, decide the night before that you will remember them. To reprogram yourself in order to remember just say to yourself several times as you begin to fall asleep, 'I will remember my dreams'. Then in the morning write down an account of your dreams immediately upon waking. If you wait until you have a cup of tea or go to the toilet you will forget. Write them down while you are still half asleep and you will remember more detail. Recall your dream by giving it the name of a made-up movie, like 'The gorilla and the pizza'. This helps you to remember as you can pick out the main topics in the dream, and write about them afterwards.

Learn from your dreams. Once you begin to record your dreams you can start to analyse them for yourself. See for instance if you can relate a part of yourself to the people in your dreams. What specific characteristics of these people are similar to your own? Forget all the dream dictionary books; you are much more aware of what a certain topic or thing means to you personally than you think. The dream diaries are useful only because they explain what the average person, or society in general, is supposed to think. If you are living magically you will realise that this is not necessary for you. Make notes of how often similar dreams occur. Ask yourself what they reflect about your life. Can you start to change the dreams? Could you influence them and end up influencing your life, giving yourself more confidence, for example? Talk through your dreams with a friend if it helps you to understand more about yourself and if it helps you to focus on the problem. Many people use dreams when they are in therapy, counselling and other types of emotional support work.

Give yourself a night of fun! Decide in advance one night that you want to go to a party, or travelling, and as you drift into sleep allow your mind to take you wherever you want. See what happens and don't forget to record it in your dream diary.

Read some of the literature available on dreaming. There are simply hundreds of books but avoid the ones that are simply dictionaries: they won't satisfy your personal growth in the long run.

Read *On Dreams: True-Life Examples of Dream Interpretation*, by Harmon H. Bro. (Aquarian, 1989), and *Living Your Dreams*, by Gayle Delaney (Harper & Row, 1988).

See also: VISUALISATION, OUT-OF-BODY EXPERIENCES, ASTRAL TRAVELLING.

Druids

Druidism is an ancient religion which focuses on oak groves and the sacredness of trees. According to myths, each priestess had a personalised tree spirit. The Greek dryads (tree nymphs) were called priestesses of Artemis, whose soul dwelt in their trees. The priestesses and priests of the druid religion, often called wizards, kept secret knowledge in their memories; they were also poets and counsellors, offering artistic and psychic wisdom to all they could.

Ireland was a place of druidism right up until 200 years ago. In order to make the story about St Patrick more acceptable to the Irish people, Catholic monks claimed that he was taught by druids. Irish churches were known as *dairthech*, or oak-house, as they were often built upon sacred oak groves.

In the early days of the religion it was matriarchal, which means woman-based, but during the revival of druidism in the eighth and ninth centuries both men and women were accepted into the faith, and men began to dominate the culture for a while. Druidic groves and evidence of worship have been found all over Europe and the Middle East as far east as Russia and the Holy Land.

Modern bigotry about earth-based religions has placed witchcraft and paganism in with druidism and called them all some demented form of devil worship without fact or evidence to back this up. There are many practising druids in Britain today.

■ *What you can do*

Some active druid cells in the UK are willing to teach and run workshops. Read as much as you can about them first. You cannot join an order such as the druids unless you are 18 or over.

Books on druidism include *The Druid Tradition*, by Philip Carr-Gomm (Element, 1991) and *The Book of Druidry*, by Ross Nichols (Aquarian, 1990).

Contact the Council of British Druid Orders or the Order of Bards, Ovats and Druids. (See ADDRESSES TO CONTACT.) Always send a stamped addressed envelope when asking for information.

See also WITCHES AND WITCHCRAFT, PAGANISM, SHAMANISM.

Earth Magic

The earth holds many mysteries and wonders. Rushing waterfalls are the source of positive energies, ancient trees hold wisdom and calmness and thunder and lightning shudder the earth with a huge bolt or force of energy. The power of a tornado or ocean wave outstretches most of what humankind can do in an instant. Many scientists talk of 'harnessing' this power, of using it for their own ends, but often this only really works when you open yourself to the magical elements of nature and the planet, including the sacred nature of the earth. It is no surprise that huge dams are collapsing, that nuclear power plants have accidents. Scientific insistence on holding and redirecting the natural flow of the earth's energies can backfire. The constant testing of nuclear weapons under the ground in the USA has put a strain on the earth and there is an increasing number of earthquakes and more extreme weather conditions. The pollution from our chemical lifestyle has also harmed our own future and that of the planet as the ozone layer is destroyed because of excess use of chlorine.

The magic of the earth has often gone unnoticed by many industrialists and scientists, who reduce everything they can to mathematical formulae and profits. Practising magic can be rewarding in itself but working with the earth, in earth magic, fulfils deep and ancient desires.

Earth magic comes in many forms. Water is the most important liquid on the planet: about 70 per cent of the earth is made from water. Water is essential to our food crops;

dolphins, fish and other creatures live in it, and it is guided by the moon. The moon's influence on water is shown primarily in the ebb and flow of the tides but we, as humans, made essentially from water (in our blood), are also affected by the moon. At the full moon suicides occur more frequently, patients in hospitals can bleed more profusely and those needing emotional or mental support may be more disturbed too.

Many waters have been sacred over the centuries; water is nearly always used to cleanse, often with salt, which represents the earth. Wells and springs can be holy and energised, and rivers can be a special source of cleansing for the whole body. The River Ganges in India is an important spiritual burial place for Hindus and in the Christian tradition, water is used to baptise children: it cleanses them, washing away their inherited 'sin'.

Fire is a symbol of destruction and rebirth, the gift of heat, light and warmth from the sky. Living flames include candles, incense and fires, which are used continuously in magic. Primitive hunters and gatherers found fire the first element they could make use of in their magic and they used it to light their way into culture and the future. The use of candlelight in magic can shift perception and awareness to a new level and create atmosphere and energy. The Mexican sun god Tezcatlipoca, or 'Smoking Mirror', is said to have transformed himself into an avatar called Mixcoatl-Camaxtle, the 'red Tezcatlipoca' to create fire for humankind.

The element earth is found in rocks and stones, in the magic transformation that changes soil and water, air and sun, into vegetation. Stone has always been important in art and spiritual culture, as a focus of devotion, like the ancient Stonehenge, or as an everlasting artefact, proof of human existence in artistic form, like the cave paintings. The earth goddess, Gaia – she who brings forth life and destroys life in the cycles of nature – is revered in every society in every time, in one depiction or another.

Air spirits represent the change in our patterns, the energy that moves and creates. Air is smell too: the scent of any living thing creates its own atmosphere, and in magical terms incense and oils are used to recreate air mystery. The wind is also a form of cleansing: it can be a gentle west wind that is soothing and healing to the powerful south wind, hot and dry. The east wind will help with matters of the head, for example if you need a clear head; it is the wind of new beginnings. The north wind is a banisher, a wind that represents death and the completion of things. The most important god in the weather system was Tesub, of Anatolian and Turkish origin. The god that produces storms and a changing climate, he always defeats the dragon of fire. He was known in Greece around 1500 BC. Notus was the Roman god of the south-west wind.

■ *What you can do*

Earth magic is powerful magic. It is around us all the time and mostly we forget to see it or hear it, yet it continues regardless.

Many ancient religions were in touch with earth mysteries and magic, which they used in rituals and myths, especially for their survival. Environmental pollution today symbolises the separation between Gaia, the great earth mother and all the gods and goddesses who watch over the earth and our survival. Practising earth magic must include protection of the earth from destruction by those who do not listen to the subtle whispers. Join an environmental group that is practising such magic, for example Dragon, ecomagic group, or the Green Circle, Applecore & Plumstone. Support others who take risks – Greenpeace, Earth First!, the Elves and others. Be aware of your own personal footprints in the earth. Do you squander and waste resources? Do you do all that you can?

Call the earth to help you in your magic and ritual. Practise your magic outside, notice the earth and what is happening to her.

Earth Mysteries and Markings

From the giant pyramids in Egypt to the massive stones of Stonehenge there are hundreds of earth mysteries on this planet whose construction and meaning lie hidden in mystery and argument.

Only after the invention of the aeroplane in 1903 did many

of the earth drawings and geometric figures in the Peruvian plains of the Nazca plateau come to life, yet they are scientifically agreed to have been constructed some 2,500 years earlier. How could people design and carry out work that was so vast and so geometrically accurate without seeing it from above? One theory, put forward in the 1960s by members of the International Explorers' Society and Jim Woodman the pilots, was that the hot air balloon was used to direct workers from above. If this were true then hot air balloons, or some form of them at least, must have been invented around 400 BC, and not in the 1780s in France, as previously thought.

This theory was tested by the Society who made a modern fabric balloon from the type of woven textiles used in 400 BC. The balloon flew – unsteadily, but nevertheless it flew. Another theory, put forward by Eric von Daniken in the 1960s, was that the Nazca drawings were the remains of landing areas used by travellers from outer space. This theory was ridiculed not least because the land itself was said to be unsuitable for landing anything heavier than the lightest of aircraft (how does anyone know how much a craft from outer space weighs?) and also because no one could agree on how these visitors would get the local people to produce drawings of their animals for the purposes of an aircraft runway.

Unfortunately this theory doesn't tell us how the giant prehistoric White Horse of Uffington in Berkshire was created and why the other representations of horses found around the south coast in England were constructed. Such giant figures, which can only be fully appreciated from the sky, have been cut into chalk hills by skilled and determined artists. One theory is that they mark places of spiritual and religious meaning. Some stories claim that they are not horses but symbols of dragons, now called horses in order to conceal their identity in an era of Christianity. The White Horse of Uffington is on Dragon Hill and has a blowing stone: if you blow through the hole a note sounds, thought to be meant to call the locals to worship. Indeed some worshippers have surmised that the figures were built by artists who could levitate whenever necessary to look over their work, or who looked on over the work in spirit form or while having out-of-body experiences.

Time is probably the only way we will know for sure, but just as we may have settled an argument about one of these megaliths or wonders, another series of earth mysteries begins.

In the 1980s a curious phenomenon was noticed in the southern part of England: crop circles. These have been found all over the south coast and now in Australia, Germany and other European countries. These are strange patterns, woven miraculously and often beautifully into the fully grown wheat and barley crops. While a good number of the circles have been exposed as hoaxes by one group of sceptics or another, the fact remains that over 3,000 such circles have been found for which scientists can find no satisfactory explanation. The newspapers and television have had a field day, exposing first one group of hoaxers then another, but claim and counter-claim aside, someone must have produced some of the circles using more than poles and bits of string. Eyewitnesses say they have been standing in the middle of fields when they felt a strange whoosh of energy and wind and the circles were formed as they stood there!

■ *What you can do*

Visit places in your area that have earth stories attached, including the mysteries of the chalk horses at Uffington, Cherhill, Alton Barnes and Westbury, and similar symbols at Wilmington, Glastonbury and Snowden Carr.

Read *Earth Mysteries* by Philip Heselton (Element, 1991) and Marian Green's *Natural Magic* (Element, 1989).

See SACRED STONES, EARTH MAGIC, DOWSING, LEY LINES.

Etheric Body

The energy that holds the psychic body together is generally called the etheric body. It represents a stage between the physical and astral forms of body and anyone who sees it might see a white, cloudy or gassy body that could look exactly like a mirror image of the real physical body. It can, with practice, be projected and become the vehicle of consciousness which can travel into many different worlds. In such cases the physical body will go into a state of deep trance, almost death-like. It is very dangerous to be woken from this state when you are travelling as you may find it difficult to get 'back in' to your physical vehicle or body.

The chakras sit in the etheric body, and they operate like a second nervous system, distributing spirit energy to the body. The etheric body never separates completely from the physical body, otherwise you would die.

See also AURA, ASTRAL PLANE, ASTRAL TRAVELLING, OUT-OF-BODY EXPERIENCES, GHOSTS.

Exorcism

Early written accounts of exorcism at work begin with Greek and Egyptian texts of about AD 500 when magicians' handbooks, beautifully copied out, suggest spells for casting out evil spirits.

Demonic or evil possession of a person has been written about in every society. Possession can last a few minutes or several years and a person who looks for religious help can expect in the most grave of cases, to have an exorcism carried out.

In Rome at the time of Jesus there were many people who specialised in exorcism, often trying to heal patients afflicted with illnesses now known to modern science and medicine as epilepsy and fits. Early exorcisms were paid affairs: one specialist in Syria is known to have charged vast amounts to calm and cast out demons from what were essentially mentally ill people. Jesus and his disciples did not charge a fee, and there are many notable and well-documented cases of exorcism throughout the Bible. Right up to the Middle Ages people were supposedly cured of possession by Christian healers who merely had to mention the name of Jesus Christ, show the sign of the cross or use the Eucharist for the demons to fly out. This could be explained by the fact that because possessed people are highly suggestible they respond easily to the idea that this or that god or sign will heal them. But the power of Christ or a similar universal energy and goodness as represented by the Eucharist carries much weight. Even today the Church carries out exorcisms but it refuses to discuss them publicly and refuses even to admit that one personality can be possessed by another.

Modern-day psychic interference by another entity can be discharged and separated, although it is unlikely that this will be done by exorcism. Possession of one soul by another is not always bad; mediums and people who undertake automatic writing, for instance, are allowing another soul to 'use' their physical body for a short time. Genuine possession is very rare and most cases that have been documented have turned out to be very sensational or untrue. The noted psychotherapist and writer, M. Scott Peck, in *People of the Lie*, admits that in recent years he has been to two successful exorcisms in which, he says that real evil, the evil which we call Satan, possessed two patients.

Exorcisms are carried out today in different ways. Ritual and some form of prayer will be involved by the person or persons carrying out the exorcism. In all cases the possessing spirit or force is 'called' away from the person or situation in which it is wrongfully placed. This practice *must only be done by someone experienced in this type of work*. It is a dangerous and difficult assignment and should only be done by those with pure, unconditional love at the core of their desire to help the person, as well as wisdom and experience of such events. Patients could die as a result of the struggle with the energy of the demon that has entered the body. The minds of those carrying out the exorcism are also at risk; it is, in effect, a brutally intense form of therapy.

Recent cases of possession seem to have common threads: an early interest in the occult, including misuse of powers and allowing spirits who were essentially 'evil' to befriend them; abuse from childhood leading to psychiatric disorders and loneliness.

The notorious film *The Exorcist* was based on the true story of a young boy who started to play with ouija boards and allowed a discarnate entity to enter his body. He lived with his grandmother and at first it was thought he was suffering from an illness or disease, but it soon became clear that he was possessed by an evil spirit, and help was sought.

■ *What you can do*

I do not recommend that you do anything other than protect and support yourself. Never allow yourself to be taken over by spirits unless you know exactly what you are doing and unless you are doing it with accredited, experienced people. Never do it if you feel uncomfortable, even if they are experts. Look first at yourself (see PERSONAL GROWTH) for ideas on how to strengthen and mature your phsychological and spiritual self.

If you are worried that you might have been possessed and need help, contact the College of Psychic Studies (see ADDRESSES TO CONTACT) or a spiritualist church representative immediately. Do not let things carry on for any length of time; always seek professional help.

Fairies

Fairies are traditionally remembered in children's story books and magical tales but there is of course a reality and history behind the stories. Fairies, like angels, elves, gnomes and brownies, kelpies and sylphs, live in the world of devic energies. This is a world often scoffed at by adults and misrepresented in stories as the fairy tales are told and retold and slightly changed for each generation.

Folklore has often interpreted fairies of any kind as dangerous, mischievous and jealous. In Ireland fairies are taken very seriously. They are respected, and often feared, and local people will know where fairy rings, fairy thorn bushes and fairy territory have been established. They will avoid these areas at all cost so they won't get possessed by the fairies and never return.

While folklore and children's stories often show fairies in a negative light, it is usually fear of the unknown and lack of respect for other beings which exacerbate these feelings.

Fairies are a very special community. There are literally thousands of different kinds of fairy. They are closely related to angels, who act as their guardians and sympathetic parents, and live essentially within the world of the unseen kingdoms. A typical garden fairy would be a small being, about two and a half feet high, made up of essentially gaseous, light colours. It seems to have no real features but from the corner of your eye you might be able to see human-like eyes and a head with a sort of mouth. Fairies can make themselves look more human, almost at will, and especially in order to communicate with us.

Fairies are very much in tune with the energies of the living plant kingdoms and their job is to tend and care for flowers, plants and shrubs. They can see the pulsing energies that come from the sun, and it is thought that they don't have to eat because the light from the sun gives them all the nourishment that they need. The way they work with flowers shows a little of how complex and unusual their job is. They will, for instance, see the light and energy coming from the sun, pulsing into the heart point of the flower, usually the bud. They are also able to see and help direct the energies and food that come from the soil. By helping these energies to merge and to establish correctly in the flower they can support its vitality.

Around the world fairies can be seen in extraordinary variety, with colours ranging from the brightest reds and greens to soft and water-like hues which give a sense of unreality. A fairy can hear colour and see sound. Fairies live on a completely different vibrational energy to ours, which is why most people cannot see them. Their world operates over and through ours. They communicate with flowers and plants through emotion, and their whole body is made up of emotional sensors.

Devas

Devas is the name given to those angelic nature spirits who have evolved over time to hold the awareness of a large area, like a field of wheat, a woodland or whole landscapes. Fairies begin life probably as the tiniest of earth fairies and then progress in their understanding and awareness of the plant kingdoms until they can fulfil the job of devas and angels. Devas know the perfect time and colour of a landscape and can consciously value and oversee the work of a particular area, from the colour of the smallest blade of grass to the connections of the colours and energies of all the plants and flowers that are in harmony around them. Their work is continuous, and because they can understand the perfect pattern and relationships of all the plants, they have a rare and all-embracing plan for the area on which they work.

Many gardeners have successfully worked with the devas of

their areas and created wonderful results. In the Findhorn community the connection with the devas and nature spirits allowed the early gardeners to create gardens of fantastical proportions from sandy, sub-standard soil. The results were huge cabbages and other vegetables which brought the community notoriety around the world. To communicate with the spirit of the nature kingdoms by connection to the devas is the highest and most unconditional form of earth magic available to a human.

■ *What you can do*

If you thought you had got past your 'childish' phase of reading about fairies, think again! Children's story books are filled with legends and tales of these beautiful creatures that live in the other world – you might want to go back and read some in light of your new understanding about them.

There are far too many fairy-tale books to mention here but keep an open mind about the way they have been written and see if you can tell a 'genuine' fairy story from a made-up version. Read *The Virago Book of Fairy Tales* and *The Second Virago Book of Fairy Tales*, edited by Angela Carter (1990 and 1992).

The easiest time to see fairies at work is probably when they are busiest, in the early morning light. They work with the light to wake up the gardens and grasses and each living thing. If you want to communicate with them, meditate and think carefully about them for as long as you can and then respect their space and feelings when you do meet up with them.

When you plant anything in your garden be aware of the relationship that the fairies and devas have in the living community outside your home. Invite them to help you in choosing the most suitable planting place, the best time to plant, the best food to offer and in caring and tending for your plant. You can get in touch with these devic energies by meditation and close attention to the plant itself.

Read Dora van Gelder's *The Real World of Fairies* (1977) and *Kingdoms of the Gods*, by Geoffrey Hudson (Theosophical Publishing House, 1970). Both are available from the Theosophical Society (see ADDRESSES TO CONTACT). For a short but philosophical introduction try William Bloom's *Devas, Fairies and Angels* (Gothic Image Publications, 1987).

Visit Findhorn community in Scotland to see and respect the nature spirits' kingdom. (See ADDRESSES TO CONTACT.)

Festivals

Society creates festivals to honour the sacred, to encourage nature and fertility, to bless and thank the dead and to speak to spirits. As time goes on many festivals and their meanings have been obscured. Christmas for example, the pre-Christian time called Yuletide, was originally a celebration of the return of the sun after the death of the old year. It was the Greek sun festival which honoured the coming of all the sun gods. The darkest days of winter were known to the Norsemen as Yule. Even the night before Christmas, 24 December, was called the Night of the Mother.

The Scandinavian god of light and joy, Baldur, according to the historian J. C. Cooper, appeared on the eve of 25 December. Santa Claus (Father Christmas) is of Germanic and Dutch origin: St Nicholas was supposed to be fond of children and give them presents. The holly, mistletoe, feasting and present-giving belong specifically to the pagan religions, and formed a part of Christmas that the Church tried unsuccessfully to ban for many centuries. All of these symbols come directly from the idea of the Divine Mother and the Divine Child.

The birth of Christ was celebrated on 6 January until the fourth century, when it was moved to 25 December. All these religious ideas have since come together for what must be the biggest celebration in the northern hemisphere each year.

The movements of the sun and moon throughout the calendar are the basis for many festivals and I have attempted to summarise the main ones here. Earth-based and other religions celebrate most of them during the year.

We are now beginning, in the New Age, to revisit these special times and to produce meaning and celebration in our lives again. Even carnivals, fêtes, fairs and pop concerts are significant gatherings that recreate at least in part a sense of community and modern culture. The next step we can take is to include these events in a more sacred way to honour ourselves and the universe.

The spiritual and celebratory year

New Year. The first full moon in February marks the Chinese New Year, Er Yue. In Celtic times the new year began on 1 November, the Samhain festival. It is now celebrated in most of the world on 1 January and marks an important point in the planting and agricultural systems for those people who live close to the land and grow food. It is regarded as the time when the dead revisit the world, and the noises of sirens, boats and bells all help to banish the old and dark and ring in the new. It is a time of spiritual purification and physical cleansing. The sun is the central part of the Hindu New Year Makar-Sankranti, which honours the Goddess of Spring.

Candlemas/Imboloc/Oimelc. Candlemas, known to pagans as Imboloc, is a major celebration of spring and light which takes place on 2 February. It is the time when the first lambs are born and ewes' milk was commonly shared. In Christianity it represents the presentation of the baby Jesus at the temple and the purification of the mother of Jesus. According to the Bible, women had to 'cleanse' themselves for forty days after having a son as the act of childbirth made them unclean (it was eighty days if you had a girl; they were supposedly twice as unclean!). The celebrations probably began at the festival of the Roman goddess Februa, who was the mother of Mars. The Celts celebrated the festival of Brigit who became the Christian St Bride, and in Ireland the celebrations, candles and light festivals still take place for this goddess of sexual fertility and fire.

Spring equinox/Eostre/Easter. This was the festival of the Saxon goddess Eostre, and the goddess Astarte from the Middle East worshipped since the Bronze Age. She was the goddess of fertility and death, recreating and destroying in the cycle of life and death. The rabbit or Easter bunny was the image of the moon hare, a sacred animal of the goddess which would lay the golden egg of the sun and fertility. For early peoples [who needed the sun and fertility to bring a good harvest,] this was an important time. Christian adoption of the festival came in the third century AD and the date is still fixed to the lunar (or moon) cycle as it always comes on the first Sunday after fourteen days of the moon as long as it is after 22 March. The festival also corresponds to the Hebrew sacrifice of the Paschal Lamb and the celebration of reincarnation with the resurrection of Christ.

Beltane/May Eve/1 May. Beltane marks the beginning of the month of Maya, the virgin Goddess of Spring, and is a traditional time to honour the earth and its fertility. The Beltane fire was lit on top of hills to mark a time of great feasting and sexual acts in Celtic traditions. Beltane was also a time when the veil between the worlds was close and communication with the fairies and nature spirits was possible. Original celebrations of May Day included dancing round the maypole or a sacred tree to celebrate the spirit of vegetation and preservation from disease. Modern May Day celebrations include the festival of workers and the beginning of the Month of Mary in the Christian tradition.

Summer solstice/Litha/21 June. When the sun was at its furthest from the equator, the time of the longest day in the northern hemisphere, it was an occasion for feasting and fires. The festivals included the Celtic sacrifice on 24 June when the Queen who is the creator sacrifices the King she bore. Druids celebrate the solstice at Stonehenge when the sun is at its highest but sadly the authorities don't allow such celebrations to go on near the stones any longer. Glastonbury has a gigantic festival at solstice time and it is definitely a time of abundance. The Japanese sun goddess Amaterasu was tempted out of her winter retreat by the sight of her face in the mirror at this time.

Lammas/Lughnashadh/2 August. Half-way between Beltane and Samhain, the Anglo-Saxon festival of Lammas welcomes the harvest. Strict observance will guarantee a wonderful crop. It is the time when the Lughnashadh fair (or festival of Lughnasa) began in Ireland, which probably originated at the time of death of King Garman. This may have been connected to the celebrations of the life of the horned and hoofed god Pan, one of the oldest gods in Greece.

Kore/autumn equinox/harvest/21–22 September. This is the time when the sun again crosses the equator and, as in the spring equinox, days and nights are of equal length giving rise to Celtic, pagan and similar festivals to honour the sun and mark the end of the harvest. In ancient Greece women honoured Thesmophoria and fertilised the seed corn with their blood for the next spring sowing. In South America women bathe each other on the seashore under the light of the moon. Kore represents water, the beginning of the rain and the darkness of winter.

Hallowe'en/Samhain/31 October. A time when the souls of the dead revisit their homes, when the veil between the two worlds is once again thin, this is the festival of the dead. Christians celebrate 1 November as All Souls' Day, but in Lithuania the pagans celebrate by sacrificing their animals to the god Zimienic who was to keep them free from the spirits of the underworld. Witches and ghosts are still associated with Hallowe'en or All Hallows' Eve, and fire is a necessary part of the celebrations.

Yule/winter solstice/21 December. Modern Yule traditions have moved to 25 December and Christmas is now celebrated even in countries with no idea of the Christian god.

Other major planetary festivals include the times of full moon and new moon, when meditations and magic work can take place. Celebrations of birth, death and marriage are also major festivals.

■ *What you can do*

Start to notice the moon! It sounds easier than it is – many people simply don't look in the sky and are unconnected with the earth's cycles.

Which festivals and feasts does your family recognise? Are you aware of their roots?

Read more to find out about the connections with such festivals and other religions and beliefs across the world. For example: *The Aquarian Dictionary of Festivals*, by J. C. Cooper (Aquarian, 1990); *Chambers Dictionary of Beliefs and Religions*

(1992); *Sacred Times – A New Approach to Festivals*, by William Bloom (Findhorn Press, 1990); *The Encyclopedia of Gods*, by Michael Jordan (Kyle Cathie, 1992); *The Women's Encyclopedia of Myths and Secrets*, by Barbara G. Walker (Harper & Row, 1983).

Gaia

The Greek name for Mother Earth or 'the deep-breasted one', Gaia represents the oldest of divinities, the ancient earth goddess.

Many religious and spiritual groups have revered Gaia as a living, breathing planet/goddess since our life here began. The beauty and complexity of our planet is still a mystery and escapes our full understanding and this has been the basis for our deep respect and reverence of the earth. Modern science and technology has tried to harness mother earth and her power with sometimes catastrophic results and our polluted planet is a testament to such greed and power.

■ *What you can do*

Respect Mother Earth. In order to live magically and spiritually within your own soul you must be conscious and aware of the energy and soul of the planet too. We are all connected; if you play your part as a cleanser rather than a polluter, the planet will benefit, and you will benefit.

Look at religious and spiritual groups who use Gaia as a basis for their beliefs, for example paganism or witchcraft.

Practise earth magic. See EARTH MAGIC, ANGELS, FAIRIES, EARTH MYSTERIES AND MARKINGS, PAGANISM, WITCHES AND WITCHCRAFT, SACRED STONES.

Ghosts

Ghosts are very different from spirits. If someone dies, for instance from a terrible accident, the physical body that the soul lives in can be reluctant to let the soul go to the spirit world or the 'other side', as it is known. It is also possible that someone who dies can choose to stay on the 'astral plane' by not recognising what's going on on the 'other side', rather like a child who wants to stay on in playschool because they don't believe that primary school exists, or that it will benefit them.

Many people who have died traumatically stay on the earth plane by accident, and they can walk around half dead and half alive for many years before they find a way out. The man in the tube station in the 1990 film *Ghost* is a classic example of a sad ghost. He had been pushed under a tube train by strangers and spent many years wandering round the underground trying to frighten the passengers just for something to do. There are many tales of soldiers, cavaliers, beheaded aristocrats and monks haunting castles and old houses.

What to do if you see a ghost:

1. Don't panic.
2. Think of the ghost as a human being who has got lost and might need help or directions.
3. Ask your guides to help you, and simply and lovingly tell the ghost that it is safe to go to the light (the spirit world). They may not have seen this light before and the energy combination of you and your guides can make it stronger for them.
4. Don't confuse ghosts with poltergeists, demons, devils or witches, and don't confuse helping them to see the light with exorcism!

Sometimes you may see someone in the spirit world who is just visiting – and your attempts to get them to see the 'light' will of course be in vain because they are already there, but they won't mind as long as you do it with the best of intentions.

Many adults will tell you that there is no such thing as ghosts or spirits. That quite simply is their business and they shouldn't stop you from believing and seeing what you can see. Many young people can see ghosts precisely because they have not closed off the part of themselves that refuses to believe in such things. In Britain, 75 per cent of the public say that they have seen some form of ghost in their lives. Why not you?

Go and watch the film *Ghost*, starring Whoopi Goldberg, for a good all-round example of what could happen. Read *The Ghost Hunters' Almanac: A Guide to over 120 Hauntings* by Peter Underwood (Eric Dobby Publishing, 1993). In fact any of Peter Underwood's books on the subject are worth getting hold of as he is one of the foremost ghost specialists in Britain.

See ASTRAL PLANE, DEATH.

Gods and Goddesses

There are gods and goddesses in every culture, for every imaginable part of life – for fertility, trees, wind, grain, sun, moon, infants, the elderly, death, creation, justice, fire, weavers, mountains, the sea, the sky, healing and fate. Just about everything you touch is blessed with the energy of a spirit god or goddess that takes care of it.

In the last 2,000 years, during the astrological time of Pisces, we have moved away from the idea of many gods and have looked towards one God as the creator of all things. This is known as monotheism and has brought with it a masculine energy that we call patriarchy. Patriarchy has served to energise and lay the foundations for a world of technology and science but at a cost to the planet, and especially to women and feminine energy. As we enter the age of Aquarius we shall be looking for the connection between God and ourselves, between our Inner God and our Universal God. This will shift and change the balance again.

Dion Fortune has written, 'all Gods are One God, all Goddesses are One Goddess, and there is One Initiator'. All gods and goddesses can be single entities but aspects of the same source, known in spirituality as the Godhead, the universal energy.

■ *What you can do*

Challenge your ideas about God: do you believe he is an old man who chastises you from above? Learn about your God within. Read the sections on MYTHS AND LEGENDS, RELIGION AND RELIGIOUS BELIEFS, REINCARNATION, UNCONDITIONAL LOVE, NEW AGE, DEATH, MEDITATION, I CHING, JESUS.

Read *The Encyclopedia of Gods*, by Michael Jordan (Kyle Cathie, 1992); *The Goddesses and Gods of Old Europe*, by Marija Gimbutas (University of California Press, 1989) and *The Language of the Goddess*, by Marija Gimbutas (Harper San Francisco, 1989).

Guardian Angels or Guides

Every single one of us, no matter how rich or poor, good or bad, how greedy or generous, has a guardian angel or guide who helps us, watching our lives with us and whispering in our ear whenever we care to listen. Along with our higher self, our guardian angels look out for us: they want the very best for our spiritual growth and for our future. They understand and accept that we have free will and they never interfere, helping us when we need help and ask for it rather than forcing us.

Guides are wise and loving beings who have chosen not to live on earth as physical beings but to support us in our choices. They are without doubt the best friends you will ever have. They know the purpose of your soul and of your lives and they will help you on your path by reminding you when they can.

■ *What you can do*

You can, through meditation and similar practices, meet your guides or guardian angels.

Sit quietly in a place where you won't be disturbed. Light a candle and ask that your guides be present with you.

Relax yourself with several deep breaths, use your favourite meditation technique and become aware of the energy around your body (your aura).

Decide that you are now lying or sitting in a beautiful meadow and feel the sunshine on your face. Look around in the meadow, touch and smell the flowers and grasses. Look into the distance and see a mountain with a castle-like building at the top. Go towards this mountain, crossing streams and climbing over hedges, through a wood, and along a path. You will reach the bottom of the mountain. Start to climb. At the door of the castle you will be met by your guide or guides. Greet them in whatever way seems appropriate and let them show you inside the castle. You can ask them questions about anything you like, you can say anything you like. Listen to their answers. Ask them their names. You might feel that you know their names instinctively or you may hear them telling you. It doesn't matter which.

Talk to your guides as long as you want, knowing that whenever you want you can return to them. Thank them and say goodbye when you have finished. Return down the mountainside and along the path, through the wood and across your streams. Find yourself back in the beautiful meadow, open your eyes and come back into your room.

Notice what happened to you on this journey, and write down as much as you can remember in your notebook. Look at how easy you made the journey itself: was the climb to the mountain castle difficult or easy? Were you tired? Elated? Full of energy?

Notice what your guide or guides looked like. Did they speak to you?

Make a note of everything that happened between you. Are you clear about the conversation?

This meditation can be repeated again and again along your spiritual path to meet your guides. At different times in your life you may need different people to help you and you will notice other guides who are there with specialist help and love (rather as we use different teachers for different subjects as we get wiser).

If you found the visualisation technique difficult then practise as much as you can; it does get easier with time. See also MEDITATION, ANGELS, VISUALISATION.

Look for spiritual guides and guardian angels in all your actions; help comes in many different ways. Expect a miracle and you will find one, expect your guides to show themselves through the good things that happen to you and the goodness in people that you meet, and they will.

Read *Living Magically*, by Gill Edwards (Piatkus, 1991).

Gurus

There have always been great women and men who have used spiritual knowledge and power to become gurus for us here on earth. The term originates from the Hindu word for spiritual teacher and a guru guides the pupil towards spiritual enlightenment and self-knowledge. The guru is called a Master in Buddhist tradition and in many other Eastern philosophies.

Many such teachers have found special purposes and possess extraordinary psychic abilities and strength, wisdom and clarity. Jesus Christ, Sai Baba, Gandhi, the Dalai Lama and Buddha are among those teachers who reached personal spiritual enlightenment and decided to share it with others.

Gurus these days can have a following of a few dozen or several million, but the teaching is the same. There are few such teachers in modern European culture, and the lack of connection to spiritual and magical values shows in the breakdown in current society.

However, as we move into the New Age of Aquarius the patterns are changing and we are said no longer to need gurus to guide us but the time has come for us to open up to our higher selves and our God within who is connected to the universal energy.

■ *What you can do*

If you want a guru to show and teach you spiritual enlightenment be wary first. Is it what you need? And is the teacher you choose ready to let go of personal power and ego to teach you? Many teachers can become so obsessed with wealth and devotion from people that it clouds their judgement and eventually destroys them. Jimmy Swaggart, the American evangelist, is a good example. He was destroyed by lust and his apparent greed for money and power.

Read the section on your HIGHER SELF. Are you ready to teach yourself on your spiritual path and recognise others who are doing the same?

Healing

There are many ways to be healed from illness other than having an operation in a hospital or going to your doctor for some tablets. A growing number of people today are looking within themselves to see what the problem is and how they themselves can utilise their bodies' own defences to help them avoid illness. They are also increasingly using alternative forms of medicine, including spiritual healing.

Healers say it is likely that 90 per cent of us can heal and are capable of channelling healing energies to another person but most of us choose not to. Particular reference is made to the young people on the earth today. It is suggested that many young people bring with them advanced healing powers and information from very old and wise souls and they have a mission to help the planet and humanity. If you are reading this book you may well be one of those people.

Holistic healing includes using medicines, although they are more likely to be natural medicines like herbs or homoeopathic remedies, but also using the mind to foster the idea of creating good health: the emotions and the physical body working together. Using psychic energy is also a form of healing and many people have found positive and startling results from being healed by people who seem to do no more than place their hands over a person's body.

Psychic or spiritual healing involves a person tuning into the energy field of their patient and directing light and energy towards them and their aura to help them reconnect those parts which are either damaged or infected. It can be an important addition to many hospitals, but so far it is only in Russia that the use of such auric healing has been taken seriously by mainstream doctors. What is actually happening in such healing is not completely understood but it is likely that the healer has the ability to direct the correct energy matrix (or jigsaw of energy) towards the patient, who then takes in this energy in order to reconstruct their own field. It is possible to reconstruct and help your own energy field without the use of outside healers purely by using the power of thought.

Britain's foremost healer, Betty Shine, explains her healing methods in detail in her book '*Mind Energy*'. It includes documentation of her work on psychic surgery where she performs psychic 'operations' on the patients, often even leaving a scar afterwards. She removes psychic rubbish that blocks the mental and physical body. After such surgery her patients have been making remarkable recoveries from their illnesses.

Most people need to be healed on a variety of levels. The work of Louise Hay shows how illness that looks as if it is physical at first can often be a giant whisper about an emotional part of your life. As your energy centre, chakras and your vital organs and body are all connected why shouldn't this be the case? For instance, according to the healer Louise Hay, acne may well be a skin illness that is found mostly in young people but it is emotionally connected to self-loathing. If this is true then the disease may be more speedily remedied by looking at the physical and psychological reasons for it together. Louise Hay recommends changing your thought patterns to introduce safety and positive energy including positive affirmations. For acne you could say, 'I love and accept myself where I am right now.'

The aura and chakras are an important part of healing, as they are directly connected to our emotional and spiritual will to live and our ability to be transformed and energised. It is sad indeed that doctors who cannot see the aura disbelieve in its existence. It is only recent scientific discovery that has led us to see and count the blood cells in our body, so in future years perhaps science will find a way to measure the aura to satisfy such sceptics. Until then we can use alternative healers to guide us towards a more holistic, all-encompassing way to heal our minds and bodies.

■ *What you can do*

Learn to heal yourself. Listen to what your body and mind is telling you about yourself. Are you aware of the negative thoughts you create yourself? Are you willing to look closely at yourself when you are ill and sort out the problem at all levels? Next time you are ill, consider visiting a healer as well as using conventional medicine. Contact the Confederation of Healing Organisations for their list of member organisations (see ADDRESSES TO CONTACT).

Read *Hands of Light: A Guide to Healing through the Human Energy Field*, by Barbara Ann Brennan (Bantam New Age Books, 1988); *Spiritual Healing*, by Jack Angelo (Element, 1991); *You Can Heal Your Life*, by Louise M. Hay (Eden Grove, 1990); and *Mind Waves*, by Betty Shine (Corgi, 1994).

Look after your body, take exercise and eat good food. You are in charge of the physical vehicle that you have chosen to use for this life: treat it as you would your favourite possession, feeding, exercising, toning, loving and cleaning it whenever possible!

Make sure that you are aware of protecting yourself, closing your aura to outside interference and illness. Many roving bacteria can enter the body because people have open auras which allow such illness to get in all too easily.

See AURAS, CHAKRAS, PROTECTION, PERSONAL GROWTH, UNCONDITIONAL LOVE and VISUALISATION.

Herbs

The practice of herbalism is as old as the herbs themselves, and they have been used over the centuries in magic, in healing and in occult practices. For those who care to look, each of the plants and blossoms here on earth has a specific and important meaning. There are records and dictionaries which cover over a thousand different herbs for all purposes.

In times past many women and men used herbs for basic healing purposes, especially as there were no doctors or hospitals to go to for sickness and accidents. It was likely that in Britain, as with many other societies, wise women who had amassed knowledge of local plants and how to use them would be called when someone was ill. This knowledge was mostly handed down from mother and daughter by word of mouth; there were few written books on such subjects. With the increasing use of allopathic medicine (as studied today) and the beginning of male power (patriarchy) in the system of healthcare, however, women's knowledge was undermined and often derided. Even so, most of the medicines we use in our hospitals today are based on the scientific properties of plants. In the Middle Ages women were burnt at the stake as witches for practising what was called 'evil magic' with herbs.

Stories of witches cutting off horsetails and mixing them with coltsfoot and shepherd's purse conjure up images of mad women boiling up bits of animals' bodies in cauldrons, yet nothing could be further from the truth. These were merely the common names of local plants; horsetail, for instance, is a plant like a fern which was used to cure kidney stones, and Native Americans use it for menstrual disorders.

There are magical uses of herbs not necessarily connected to healing, and some herbs when drunk could even affect the body and mind in such a way as to inspire and produce hallucinations, trances and altered states of consciousness, rather like the drugs we use today.

The most famous herbalist of modern times is Culpeper and it is still possible to buy volumes of his work describing herbs and their use in everyday life.

■ *What you can do*

As most herb books contain information on those herbs commonly used in healing and eating, listed here are some details about the types of herbs used in rituals, psychic and spiritual work from Paul Beyrel's excellent *Master Book of Herbalism*, now sadly out of print.

Before using herbs here are a few golden rules:

1. Always know where your herbs have come from. Don't buy them from sources that could have used pesticides and similar chemicals.
2. Grow them yourself if you can, tending them with

affection and calling on the nature spirits to help take care of them (see FAIRIES).
3. Picking them at full moon for spiritual work is a good idea, simply because any plant or flower will be at its most potent at this time.
4. Make sure all your equipment, whether it be pans and jars for infusing or pestle and mortar for crushing, is clean both physically and psychically. Use ritual salt water and heat.
5. Use mistletoe wood for the handles of any knives used for cutting, or at least wooden handles if you can't get mistletoe.
6. Make a note of the herbs and uses as you go along and the effect they had/experiences you had for next time, to build up knowledge and patterns.

Herbs used for spiritual and psychic work

To bless a house. Mix camphor and basil in with the cleaning water in a new house. Plant basil for protection as soon as you move in. Put dill-seed in bread and cakes for a housewarming party. Add elderflower blossoms to a shared punch. Hang mistletoe at Christmas with a red ribbon to encourage protection, good luck and love.

To purify. For spiritual meditation and to cleanse the body use angelica in the bath, burn basil and drink it with blessed thistle as a tea with a little honey. Drink sage to clear your mind of negative thoughts and burn frankincense as an incense for rituals and meditation.

To honour the dead. Bury mandrake root with the body to protect the spirit on its journey. Plant parsley on the site of the grave. Drink tea with chervil to encourage communication with the soul and to guide the soul to the other planes. Always put bluebells on the grave to bring peace and blessings.

For weddings. Decorate with meadowsweet, ivy, roses and rosemary. Make a ritual cup to drink with coriander, mistletoe berries, orchid roots, rosemary and anise seed. Let the couple jump over the shrub broom to symbolise their new life together.

Read *A Modern Herbal*, by Mrs Grieve (Penguin, 1980), and *Herbal Medicine*, by R. F. Weiss (Beaconsfield Press, 1988).

Contact the National Institute of Medical Herbalists for a directory of herbalists in your area. Write to Potters (Herbal Supplies) for a free booklet on herbal remedies. (Enclose a large SAE.) Write to the School of Herbal Medicine if you wish to become a serious student. (See ADDRESSES TO CONTACT.)

Higher Self

Your higher self, your inner guidance, your God within, is the most wise and loving part of yourself. It represents the essence of your soul and your connection to the universe of the Godhead. The more we live magically, spiritually, the more we get in touch with our higher selves.

When Carl Jung, the psychoanalyst, was treating patients with symptoms of multiple personalities he found that at least one of the so-called sub-personalities in many of the patients was of a much higher consciousness and displayed a wisdom and clarity that was not found in the others. This has also been found by other specialists and there seems to be a growing understanding that there is a part of our consciousness, beyond our subconscious, that exists.

Our higher selves have access to all the answers that we need to know about ourselves and our future, about our present and past. Your higher self is the best teacher and guru you will find.

■ *What you can do*

Meet your higher self. Prepare yourself over a number of weeks or even months. Learn to meditate and prepare a 'space' in your mind whenever you meditate for when you meet your higher self. As your connection to yourself and your spiritual awareness grows you will find yourself coming closer to meeting your higher self. Learn to listen to your higher self. When you open up to the whispers and clues that you are given every day about yourself and the things you do you will be living magically.

Read *Living Magically*, by Gill Edwards (Piatkus, 1991).

See MEDITATION, GODS AND GODDESSES, GUARDIAN ANGELS OR GUIDES, ANGELS, PERSONAL GROWTH, VISUALISATION.

Hypnosis

Hypnosis is now readily used in the medical and emotional treatment of smokers; adults who have suffered from childhood sexual abuse; fears and phobias of many kinds, but little is really known about the powers of the hidden mind, even today.

In the late eighteenth century, Franz Anton Mesmer became interested in magnetic therapy, known then as 'animal magnetism'. He believed, through the influence of the sixteenth-century German alchemist Paracelsus, that the universe and planets influenced human beings through magnetism. In 1778 in Paris he was treating hundreds of people with common ailments in a star-studded showbiz-type atmosphere. He would dress as a magician and play soft music to his patients while a tub of iron filings, representing magnets was in the centre of the room. It was only after more work and experiments were done, that he found the magnets were of no relevance whatsoever, and that he had inadvertently discovered hypnotism.

Two English doctors took up the challenge for more practical use and used hypnosis to anaesthetise patients during serious and painful operations. Unfortunately for them, chloroform was invented at about the same time and the doctors were never taken seriously even though they managed to saw off the legs of patients without pain!

When he was a medical student, the psychoanalyst Freud saw hypnosis being used to induce hysteria and freakish incidents and the experience made a marked impression on him; indeed, it became the basis for his studies and theory of the unconscious and the power of dreams.

The hypnotic state can also be used to induce a deeper and more marked psychic awareness and to heighten the ability to experience unusual phenomena, most specifically, telepathy. Brain-scan activity is apparently changed when under hypnosis and the body and mind is definitely more relaxed. Charles Honorton and Rex Standford published the most impressive studies about the psychic abilities of people under hypnosis, including using ESP card guessing games. In the studies carried out more than 50 per cent of people were more efficient when under hypnosis, allowing the investigators to conclude that if you want to increase your chance of being psychic then get hypnotised!

The hypnotic state has been closely observed by governments. The Russian government, for example, funded and carried out extraordinary work in the Commission on Hypnotism and Psychophysics even to the point where exiled Russian chess players have claimed that they are instructed in the rudiments of hypnosis and extrasensory perception as a matter of course.

What does seem to happen is that you can get in touch with your higher self which has an extraordinary capacity to achieve anything, feel anything and guide you to improved health and success.

■ *What you can do*

Self-hypnosis is possible but not recommended to a beginner. What is interesting to learn from all this is that a relaxed state of mind and body will probably increase your chance of having a psychic experience if you want one. See MEDITATION.

Hypnosis can be carried out on a grand scale, but as with the television and showbiz personalities today, this is only really for light entertainment. To really feel the positive benefits of hypnosis treatment, for phobias for instance, always contact a reputable person, preferably one who is recommended or used by healing institutes.

Read *The Hypnotic World of Paul McKenna* (Faber & Faber, 1993) for a good insight and explanation of hypnosis.

See HIGHER SELF.

I Ching

The Chinese *I Ching*, or *Book of Changes*, records the oldest and most complex of all known forms of divination. It has been used over centuries by politicians and emperors, by queens and kings and by all manner of enquirers who search for answers to complex problems.

The first emperor of China, Fu Hsi, is credited with the invention of the *I Ching* and it was further developed by King Wen, first ruler of the Chou dynasty in 1143 BC. The system has been developed strictly according to spiritual and cosmological principles, which enable its development slowly to build up deep philosophical understanding of the enquirer using obscure and difficult texts and language. It has been said that the system itself is so complicated that it has its own sense of humour and personality.

The basic *I Ching* comes from the meaning and interpretation of yang and yin, the two complementary opposites representing male and female; odd and even; light and darkness; yes and no; day and night; plus and minus and other dualities. Yang is depicted within the *I Ching* as a solid, single line ⎯⎯ and Yin is a broken line in two pieces ⎯ ⎯. The *I Ching* was devised from studying these lines and the relationship that they had to all living and non-living things in the world. The lines were used to create the eight basic trigrams listed here:

☰ called Ch'ien which represents heaven, daytime, sky and the creative energy in all things. It means a definite change for the better and the three unbroken lines show vitality, good luck and strength. It is connected to the head and mind, and associated with early winter and oncoming icy weather. In the family it is linked to the father.

☷ K'un represents the earth, the mother, femininity and the womb. As the exact opposite of Ch'ien, it represents the ultimate in female energies or yin, which is yielding dark and nourishing. It is connected to early autumn and warmth and night-time.

☳ Chên is the movement and thunder and development of all things. The two broken lines indicate change and the apprehension or coming fear of change, including excitement and earthquakes. It is a representation of expansive energy and spring and the first son.

☵ K'an, is the sign for danger and is connected with the mind and concentration. It also relates to flowing water, and the unbroken line in the centre is a sign of inner strength. It is a sign of anxious people and represents midwinter and cloudy skies and the second son.

☶ Kên shows blocked actions, either by a mountain in the way or by a short rest during a process. It is a representation of late winter and stillness, also stubbornness and the third son.

☴ Sun is the representation of the wind and the wood, which in turn shows movability and influence and the growth of natural matter. It is gentle and gradual and represents early summer and the first daughter.

☲ Li means separation but also firmness and beauty and the second daughter. It is consciousness and dependability, but the sun, fire and lightning are also connected.

☱ Tui is a representation of happiness, satisfaction and joy, including the achievements and progress of a project or aim, the third daughter and in nature by a lake.

These eight trigrams are only the beginning of this system. To consult The *I Ching* for yourself read one of the many books available.

All popular versions of the *I Ching* in Britain derive from *The I Ching*, or *Book of Changes*, the Richard Wilhelm translation rendered into English by Cary F. Baynes (foreword by C. G. Jung), Routledge & Kegan Paul, 3rd edition, 1968. The best long English version to read is *The I Ching Workbook*, by R. L. Wing (Aquarian Press, 1990) or *I Ching: The Book of Changes*, by Thomas Cleary (Shambhala, 1992).

This system of divination is highly revered throughout the world and has been used for many centuries so successfully that even when the communist leader Mao Zedong rejected other esoteric traditions he left the *I Ching* intact, primarily, he claimed, because it worked. Centuries earlier the Chinese philosopher Confucius said that if he had had another fifty years to live he would have devoted them all to the study of the *I Ching*.

See also DIVINATION, MAGIC, TAROT CARDS, BUDDHISM.

Incense and Oils

For thousands of years we have used smell to create magic, mystery and atmosphere. Formulas, potions, remedies and brews have been passed down from generation to generation by word of mouth, by secret signs, by codes locked up in spellbooks. Incense and oils have played a major role in the magic of natural medicine for the mind and body over many thousands of years.

The key thing to remember when using incense and oils for magical work is that they contain an energy of their own and it is when you mix in the power of your thought and the power of your intent with this energy that you can create magic. By combining the special energies of the chosen oils and the power of your thought the mixture can increase its potency and be more effective.

Incense has been used for probably the longest time, beginning with ancient rituals when priests and priestesses would burn herbs and resins together to purify the air before prayers, to mask the smell of the skin of animals that were being sacrificed and to produce an atmosphere suitable for such spiritual work. Today, many churches still use incense burnt on charcoal blocks during special ceremonies, and in the Roman Catholic and Jewish traditions the ritual burning of frankincense and myrrh began with the birth of Jesus and the gifts from the Magi.

Originating in the Far East, incense sticks have now become widely available and they are sold all over the world in vast quantities. In countries like India they can be used daily to ward off evil spirits and mosquitoes at the same time!

What makes the difference is the oil or resin you choose. For incense that you prepare yourself the commonest ingredients are pine needles (for purification, money and healing); rose petals (for love and sexual desire!); rosemary (to awaken the body, add love and healing); frankincense (to increase spiritual awareness); cinnamon (for money and psychic awareness, but use carefully) and sandalwood (for healing massage and meditation). You can mix many different oils and herbs together in a bottle to make a personal incense. Many shops now sell oils and herbs already made up in bottles and bags but it's always more fun and often cheaper to make your own.

■ *What you can do*

Here are some recipes for the most commonly used oils and incense:

To attract love. Burn one part cinnamon, one part cedar, one part rose petals and two drops of cypress oil on a charcoal block.

To aid studying. Burn either benzoin resin or mastic gum with lavender and sage and two drops of basil oil. Alternatively, burn two drops of basil oil on an oil burner with two drops of lavender.

To help you sleep. Mix two drops of rose oil, two drops of jasmine or jojoba oil with one drop of camomile in a small bowl of pure almond or olive oil. Mix well and rub on the soles of the feet, and wrists.

For sexual energy. Mix one drop of cardamom, one drop of sandalwood, two drops of patchouli and ginger and one drop of clary sage.

Always remember: Never put concentrated oils on your skin, always mix first with a good-quality base oil. Don't let the oils sit in sunlight and don't store them in plastic bottles: they will become less potent very quickly.

Always burn incense on a proper burner. Charcoal burns at a high temperature and will be extremely dangerous unless it is carefully placed on non-flammable material. Never let the burner get too hot and have a pair of oven gloves and glass of water ready for emergencies. Never let the incense burn when you have left the room and don't throw hot charcoal into the dustbin where it could ignite other materials.

Read *The Complete Book of Incense, Oils and Brews* by Scott Cunningham (1991) and *Cunningham's Encyclopedia of Magical Herbs* (1985) both published by Lewellyn New Times Books, and *The Joy of Aromatherapy*, by Cathy Hopkins (Angus & Robertson, 1991).

For an up-to-date list of aromatherapists contact the International Federation of Aromatherapists (see ADDRESSES TO CONTACT).

Jesus

The word 'magic' comes directly from the Magi, the three wise men of the East who took gifts of frankincense, gold and myrrh to the infant Jesus in Bethlehem. When Jesus was older he was considered by many to be a magician. In AD 180 the writer Celsus wrote a raving attack on Christianity based on this premiss, saying that Jesus had learnt his magic in Egypt.

But it is unlikely that Jesus was a magician. The publicity he got at the time was enough to secure a huge following wherever he went anyway, and Christianity has survived until today because of the stories of the ability of Jesus to produce magical effects like turning water into wine, healing the sick and bringing back the dead to life, walking on water and casting out evil spirits. It is much more likely that this extraordinary spiritual teacher was gifted with many healing and psychic abilities. Even many of the most ardent non-believers in psychic phenomena will often defend the miracles of Jesus Christ without question.

The Bible is an amazing account of this man who used his inner self to show us that unconditional love could conquer all things, and that we are all sons and daughters of God. Nothing in this book disagrees with anything that Jesus has offered us. Only a frightened and narrow-minded interpretation of life and of Christianity has kept us away from realising and believing in the existence of the miracles of Jesus and listening closely to his messages. Jesus told us everything that we still disbelieve – that life exists after death, that we can cure each other with love, that when we hurt someone else we are hurting ourselves, that we are all connected closely together through the universal energy of the Godhead. That everything is possible.

The Christ energy, or the invocation of the spirit of Jesus Christ, is one of the most powerful energies known to combat and change evil. The Christ energy (often called the Cosmic Christ) represents unconditional love in its purest form, and this energy supports the universe by healing, purifying, redeeming and balancing. This is why this energy is often used and called on so successfully in cases of psychic attack, exorcism and similar problems.

■ *What you can do*

Don't turn off Jesus just because of modern Christianity. Read the Gospels of Matthew, Mark, Luke and John in the Bible as if you were reading an autobiography of a special man with extra-ordinary abilities. What do you think it would be like if Jesus was here today saying the same thing?

Jung

Carl Jung was born in Switzerland in 1875 and was a student and collaborator of Sigmund Freud and his work. Carl's mother, Emilie, was an occultist and his father a minister. In his childhood he was allowed to explore and realise his strange dreams and experiences. Throughout his life Carl Jung witnessed many extraordinary psychic happenings, most of which he kept secret until later years when he thought they might be more acceptable to society.

Jung's main work was that of dream interpretation. In this field he was to outshine Freud, whose interpretations of dreams as mainly sexual and childhood orientated Jung eventually thought to be limited and obscure. After his break from Freud in 1913 Jung began to have vivid and uncontrollable dreams. For a period of six years he was depressed but studied his depression and his dreams in detail, even producing stunning paintings of some of his visions. It is because of all this work that modern analysis of dreams and dream interpretation has evolved and been used in psychoanalysis and psychiatry. Jung saw its power. He also witnessed other worlds, outside is own and he met and spoke to people in his dreams who, he claimed, were from other dimensions or planes of existence.

While all this was going on Jung himself was experiencing strange phenomena in his own house. He claims that he could feel his rooms full of spirits, that his daughter saw a woman in a white dress walking through the room, that another child had her bedclothes taken from her bed while she was in bed asleep, and seemingly meaningless poltergeist-type tricks were played for many months upon the whole family. It wasn't until 1950 that he related the stories of his personal experiences with spirits and ghosts in his work, *Ghosts: Reality or Delusion?*

Carl Jung was also interested in another important tool for those interested in spiritual occultism, the *I Ching*. He confessed in 1950 that he had been consulting the *I Ching* for over thirty years.

Jung was responsible for naming our current understanding of the 'collective unconscious'. This was the idea that myths, folklore and ideas had a common understanding in societies, beyond our personal subconscious mind. Jung called them 'archetypes' and named them, for instance, the Wise Old Man, the Great Earth Mother. This has made an important contribution to society's understanding of ourselves and our mythological past.

■ What you can do

Jung's books are fairly hard work for the uninitiated, so try to get hold of readers and shorter interpretations if you are interested in following this up. Classic works include the autobiographical *Memories, Dreams, Reflections*, the *Red Book* and *Man and His Symbols* (Arkana Press, 1989).

Jung believed that every dream could hold a message and that to find the message you just had to look closely enough.

See DREAMS, I CHING.

Karma

Karma is the name given to the process that each of us goes through in our lives when our actions are followed by consequences. The idea of karma originally came from the Hindu religion and it is a central part of Buddhist philosophy. Karma is also closely related to reincarnation. What you do in this life counts: if you have lived a good life, one of service and spiritual wealth, you will have built up good karma for your next life. On a simplistic level the basic laws of magic apply – if you create bad magic, you will attract bad magic; if you create good, then you will attract good.

In both Buddhist and Hindu philosophy the creation of good karma is the key to spiritual enlightenment.

■ *What you can do*

Search within yourself and evaluate your own karmic energy. Are you proud and aware of the consequences of your actions? Do you think they will be valued as attracting good karma or bad towards yourself?

Read the sections on REINCARNATION, MEDITATION, DEATH, BUDDHISM and PERSONAL GROWTH for more information.

Ley Lines

The first person in the modern world to name the strange energy lines that ran across Britain was Alfred Watkins in the early 1920s. The Victorians, however, had already noticed that many ancient sites, including Stonehenge and Avebury, were in alignment with each other and with other boundaries and markings.

The lines denote the earth lines of magnetism and can be picked up by good dowsers. It is thought that they were first known in the Bronze Age and mystic and spiritual places have been traced back as far as archaeologists have found prehistoric remains. It seems that when the lines have been identified, rather like the meridian 'energy' lines in Chinese acupuncture on the body, they have been used for many thousands of years as places where people who knew and understood them have built their temples, churches and megaliths, like Stonehenge. When Watkins discovered them in 1921, at first he thought that they were merely paths for trading, but a cursory glance at a few of the better-known lines cast doubt on this theory.

Now it is commonly recognised that the lines could be straight energy paths on which major and minor constructions of spiritual and mythical interest were built to 'harness' or make good use of their energy.

Ley lines exist all over the world. They have been discovered in Bolivia, and the Nazca Lines in Peru pass over hills and valleys for six miles. They are known in South America as *tak'is*, meaning straight lines of holy places and spirit paths.

A high incidence of psychic phenomena is said to have taken place along ley lines and people have reportedly experienced re-enactments of battles, levitation, UFOs and similar phenomena.

■ *What you can do*

Ley lines can be picked up by infra-red photography and also by good dowsers but they can be almost exactly mapped simply on a large Ordnance Survey map.

If you are interested in discovering lines in your local area, start by buying a good Ordnance Survey map size 1:50,000 and look for likely points. You could go to the highest point in your town or village and look closely around. What can you see? Look for clues like churches, beacons, stones, crosses and even yew trees. Start collecting evidence and visit your local library; they will always have older maps and you can trace the development of your area for at least the last few hundred years.

Visit your local history or archaeological society and also check for local stories, myths and legends. As well as being a helpful source of information on the lines they are always fascinating. Keep good records and notes of your discoveries. Read Philip Heselton's excellent book, *Earth Mysteries* (Element, 1991).

Magic

The most basic form of magic is about change. Change can consist of using nature and the natural elements to energise or aid an individual into changing something about their lives. It can use mysticism, spells, meditation, whispers, oils and herbs, crystals, divination, psychic powers, healing and alternative states of consciousness.

Magic is a mixture of religion and science. A 'magical cure' for instance can be the prayers of one woman coupled with the healing power of the herbs and poultices laid on a wound or injury. In medieval times it was the witches who used natural magic to help others. Similar 'magic' was being carried out in every country in the world but only in Europe and the USA were women burned to death or drowned for practising it (see WITCHES AND WITCHCRAFT).

To live magically is the most beautiful thing available to your soul. Everything is perfect and open to change; you create your destiny and your dreams and the more you focus on what you want the more likely it is that you can find magical elements in your life at every turn. Our lives are never meaningless or random; when we can see that everything that happens to us is part of the reality that we have created we can see it as a magical dream, created by us, for us.

Change doesn't have to be painful either, although many people start to be conscious of spiritual or magical issues through pain, perhaps when someone close to them dies.

To choose change is powerful. You may well begin to look

at magic thinking you can settle an old score or get even with someone, or you might think that you can attract a certain person towards you for love, but without fail people who practise this kind of magic find that the lesson comes back on them and they must learn, or lose their power. Practising so-called 'black magic' with intent to cause harm or pain is stupid and dangerous, not only for the recipient but for yourself. You can unlock a force of negative energy whose effects you will not be able to control. People who practise black magic don't last long.

Positive magic is also powerful, but the snowball effect that it has on your life is far more important to your spiritual growth. Before practising positive magic, agree the basic rules: create magic from a desire to love and create happiness, never harm another being, never misuse magic.

When you use spirituality to get in touch with yourself you can find that you have magic within you. Everyone has an inner teacher (see HIGHER SELF) that can help unfold the special magic within.

Magic also represents the unknown. Just think that 2,000 years ago there were gods and goddesses of tides, the moon, air and fire. Natural elements have today taken on a much more scientific meaning and they have 'lost their magic', but there are some natural occurrences that are simply not explained even now. Using the moon, water, fire and earth you can connect with nature to energise your will and desires, thus creating magic.

■ *What you can do*

Practise magic every day – look for opportunities to learn and change. Get to know the natural magical forces of energy and work towards understanding and living in harmony with them. See EARTH MAGIC.

Imagine you have rainbows spreading out from the palms of your hands and that you could 'direct' them at people you choose in order to help. Notice what happens to the other person or thing. Does it help?

Treat every single thing that happens to you for a week as magic.

Write it all down, look for connections, look to see if your inner teacher, or higher self has been trying to tell you something. Treat it as if you are in a dream where you can make people happy or sad around you, and see what happens. Use your rainbow energy.

Read books about practical magic, to attract loving people towards you for instance, or to heal a friend, pass an exam or get on better with your parents.

Read *A Witch Alone: Thirteen Moons to Master Natural Magic*, by Marion Green (Aquarian, 1991); *Natural Magic*, by Marion Green (Element, 1989); *Stepping into the Magic* (1993) and *Living Magically* (1991), by Gill Edwards, published by Piatkus Books; *The Complete Book of Incense, Oils and Brews*, by Scott Cunningham (Llewellyn, 1991).

For a historical perspective read *Egyptian Magic*, by E. A. Wallis Budge (Arkana, 1988); *A History of Magic*, by Richard Cavendish (Arkana, 1990); *The Women's Press Book of New Myth and Magic*, edited by Helen Windrath (Women's Press, 1993); *Earth Power: Techniques of Natural Magic*, by Scott Cunningham (Llewellyn, 1983); and *Magic and the Magician*, by W. E. Butler (Aquarian, 1991).

Make yourself a magic wand from 40 centimetres of straight hazel bush, cut at the full moon. Peel the bark and ritually send your energy into the wand. Cap the end with silver or golden foil and make special, personal markings and symbols at each end. Use the wand to throw rainbows, to direct energy into herbs, oils and plants, for spells and to send love.

Meditation

Meditation has a number of benefits, taking it beyond the 60s image of weirdos dressed in white flowing clothes. Today, meditation forms the basis for most spiritual work, and for many it is also an important form of relaxation and stress reduction.

Meditation can help you unwind after a difficult day, it can help you learn to see things from many perspectives, build up your self-esteem and respect for yourself and overcome desperate feelings. Modern counsellors often use guided meditations to release fears and anger about pasts events and to understand their clients better.

Visualisation is the art of creating pictures in your head. These pictures, or visual images, are very powerful and can dramatically change your life for the better. Using creative visualisation when you meditate helps you to concentrate on the story in hand and forget what you are going to have for lunch! Start by picturing a daffodil or rose in your hand, bring it close to you and smell it, look at the colour, the leaves, any insects or blemishes on it. If you can do this, you can easily prepare yourself for visualisation during meditation.

There are many meditation techniques, some more powerful than others, and there are many religious groups who advocate one or other of these special practices. A current popular version uses relaxation and visualisation rather than a technique like transcendental meditation. Listening to, or watching the breath is a standard technique which sounds very simple, but try doing only that for a full five minutes without your mind wandering!

It is common to use a candle, a beautiful picture or pattern or even a point in space so that you fix your eyes on this image and then relax all your body while keeping your spine straight. The spine is important: you need to make sure the energy travelling through your body does so easily and that your chakras are in position. Imagine that your spine is actually a pile of pennies and that you are trying to get them all to line up on top of each other. Many people sit either cross-legged or on a chair to make this easier. You should also make sure that your feet or the base of your spine are placed firmly on the ground; this will help to 'earth' you so that your energy doesn't drift away. It is especially important when you first start to meditate as your personal energies may well be out of balance with yourself and you could feel dizzy. If you feel sick or dizzy during meditation, stop! Run your hands under the cold tap, drink a cup of tea, stamp your feet on the ground and mentally imagine that your aura is protected by a 'bubble' which allows nothing harmful inside it. If you still feel sick then you should get professional help. A small number of people find that they cannot balance themselves during meditation, and they should find help immediately.

One popular type of meditation is chanting a 'mantra'. This technique uses a sound or chant which becomes the focus for the meditator, like looking at the candle flame. You whisper the word, like *Om* (this means connection to God) slowly until you can think the word without moving your lips; imagine hearing it without speaking. Concentrate on a small word like *Om* to take your attention into the right place for clearing the mind.

Transcendental meditation was introduced into Europe in the 1960s by Maharishi Mahesh Yogi. It consists of meditation that uses a personally given mantra that is repeated time after time, often causing a trance-like effect. The meditation itself has been scientifically measured and is said, like other forms of meditation, to lower blood pressure and slow down the heart rate.

■ *What you can do*

Learn to meditate. It is the basis of all good spiritual and psychic work, as reading the other sections of this book will prove.

See also VISUALISATION.

Read *The Inner Guide to Meditation*, by Edwin Steinbrecher (Aquarian, 1982); *The 3 Minute Meditator*, by David Harp (Piatkus, 1990); *Meditation: the Inner Way*, by Naomi Humphrey (Aquarian, 1987); *Creative Visualization*, by Ronald Shone (Thorsons, 1984); and *How to Meditate*, by Lawrence LeShan (Crucible/Aquarian, 1989).

Look for classes, sanctuaries, even churches, where you can meditate and learn with others.

Start your own meditation group if you can't find one near you.

Mediums

A medium is a person who is sensitive to subtle forms of energy and atmosphere that cannot be reached by our five senses of touch, smell, hearing, sight and taste.

These energies are sensed and translated through the medium's mind, often carrying the force of the personality of the spirit concerned. They will be recounted either through the voice of the medium or through drawing or painting.

Mediums have the ability to tune up and raise their

vibrational energy to see and communicate with energies and spirits which normally operate on a higher frequency in the other worlds; they use trance or meditation to achieve this state, as the body must be relaxed and comfortable. The aura and chakras play the most important part in this communication as these are the source of the energy from which the psychic centres are activated and protected.

Mediumship is a vocation, a serious decision for anyone to take. It is not about sitting in a darkened room waiting for a voice to come through. Being a medium involves a person declaring to work in tandem with their spirit guides and in the process learning and developing themselves to work for the greater good of the universe. There are very few places to learn, and some mediums find that they lose confidence quickly when people ridicule or disbelieve them. Often they have simply not understood or properly used the relationship between themselves and their spirit. They may have picked up messages from their subconscious, emotional self, their higher self and their spirit guides. Often these messages may seem confused or garbled. It is likely that the inexperienced medium has simply not got the whole message.

Another problem with some mediums is that they can think that the spirit is an all-knowing, all-intelligent being. Spirits will have a very much more open and knowledgeable understanding of the other worlds, but not all of them are developed enough to communicate or use this knowledge. If you communicate with your dead Auntie Madge or Uncle Bill there is no reason to believe that she or he could really tell you very much more than they could when they were alive. Of course, people are greatly encouraged when they do communicate with lost ones: it can offer hope and understanding of reincarnation and life after death.

One of today's great British mediums, Ivy Northage, channels her spirit guide, Chan, to public audiences all over the country. (Dates and venues can be obtained from the College of Psychic Studies): see ADDRESSES TO CONTACT. Chan has spoken and taught spiritual ideas for many years through the body of Ivy Northage, who says that she wasn't looking for this work but the signs and whispers she received were so very strong that she could not ignore them. Highly evolved spirit guides such as Chan work with a medium to communicate ideas and teachings to those who will listen. The work is often sensitive and loving; real guides don't have to tell you what to do, they teach you to realise for yourself what you have to do.

The main reason why people visit mediums is to talk to friends or relatives who have died. This can be a positive or disappointing experience, depending on who you see.

■ *What you can do*

If you want to be a medium, start to prepare yourself now. Knowledge of the chakras, the aura, various levels of ESP, meditation and personal growth are all important.

The more developed you are as an individual soul, the more you will be able to achieve and the stronger your ability will be when working with spirit guides. You are likely to pick up and communicate with spirit guides who are on your own level and whom you can 'resonate' with in terms of energy.

Attend classes and watch mediums at work, either through the Spiritualist Association of Great Britain or the College of Psychic Studies (see ADDRESSES TO CONTACT). Always make sure that you are learning with someone you can trust and that you feel safe with. Always be in control of your own body and learn to close down your chakras after any form of psychic activity.

See also CHANNELLING, PERSONAL GROWTH, AURA, CHAKRAS, DEATH. Read *Mediumship Made Simple*, by Ivy Northage (Psychic Press, 1986); *Mediums and their Work*, by Linda Williamson (Robert Hale, 1990); and *Mind to Mind*, by Betty Shine (Corgi, 1989).

Don't expect too much from a medium. If they are good they will be able to get an idea of how your deceased friend or relative is feeling but often there isn't much to say at all other than how happy or unhappy they are now. The perspective from the spiritual world is obviously different to ours, and many things are simply not important any more.

Beware of mediums who charge large amounts of money and are not already connected to or recommended by reputable groups and organisations. You may be wasting time and effort talking to someone who cannot possibly get in touch with your loved ones, no matter how much they try. Go by your instinct – if a medium feels dodgy to you, then don't do it.

Read *Spirit Speaks* and *Soul to Soul* magazines. Channelled information and teachings from the spirit world. See MAGAZINES.

Myths and Legends, Folk Tales and Fables

People need a story, an idea of why they are here and what they expect from life and the universe. We use these myths to tell us how to live, to learn morals and to stimulate our emotions. In mythology we create culture and poetry, use our intellect and imagination. Mythology gives us a story for natural events and occurrences that we cannot understand. It gives us personal meaning and explanation without science. Mythology lives in the spiritual plane of our mystical consciousness.

Because mythology comes from another plane of existence the functions are often sacred. The renowned mythologist and historian, Joseph Campbell, said in *The Hero of One Thousand Faces*, 'myth opens the world to the dimension of mystery, to the realization of the mystery that underlies all forms. If mystery manifests through all things, the Universe becomes a holy picture.'

Throughout history, societies have created myths and stories which essentially are very similar. Campbell, who studied the subject all his life and worked with the analyst Jung, collected thousands of stories originally passed down by word of mouth. His huge volumes of work on mythology read, as he calls it, like the rhythm of life. Whether you read the Greek myths, derived largely from Homer, or the work of Blake or Shakespeare, the stories of the Native American Indians, or Celtic myths of King Arthur and his knights, the similarities of the struggle for personal recognition and spiritual enlightenment, between good and evil, to overcome physical difficulties are there. All religions use mythology to assert their culture.

Today's heroes and myths are created more often in the movie world. My favourite films are those by Steven Spielberg, who produces spiritual mythology in *Close Encounters of the*

Third Kind, *ET*, *Indiana Jones* and *Always*. They all tell universal, spiritual stories in such a way that if you didn't know about reincarnation, for instance, it wouldn't matter.

Many theologians and philosophers believe that the loss of an unacceptable modern mythology in society stresses young people to breaking point. The world is moving and changing so quickly that the old stories are no longer relevant. With the dawning of the next century and the New Age of consciousness, we have to reinvent mythology for ourselves and to understand our connection to the universe.

■ *What you can do*

Mythology is a powerful subject. If you want to be stimulated – get reading! Try Joseph Campbell's *The Hero of a Thousand Faces: The Power of Myth* (Bollinger, 1949); *The Illustrated Encyclopedia of Myths and Legends*, by Arthur Cotterell (BCA and Marshall Editions, 1989); *Greek Myths*, by Robert Graves (there are many different editions of this, including an illustrated version by Cassell, 1985); *The Golden Bough*, by J. G. Frazer (Papermac, 1987); *Personal Mythology: the Psychology of Your Evolving Self*, by David Feinstein and Stanley Krippner (Unwin Paperback, 1989).

Discover the mythology of your own life. What stories are passed down in your religion, traditions, from your grandparents and schools?

See RITUALS, GODS AND GODDESSES, RELIGION AND RELIGIOUS BELIEFS, DEATH.

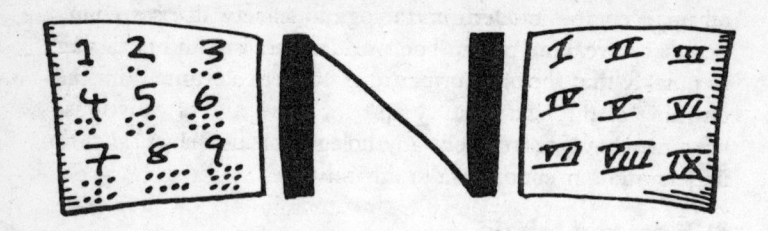

Near Death Experiences

NDE (near death experiences) occur when a living person comes close to death, or in some cases actually dies, but survives to tell the tale. These experiences obviously vary but they are often connected with people who have accidents or are in hospital under anaesthetic or in serious trouble like cardiac arrest.

Studies have been carried out in many cases of NDE with children who tell a remarkably similar tale; that of light and a feeling of well-being and goodness. Dr Melvin Morse, in his bestselling book, *Closer to the Light: Learning from the Near Death Experience of Children*, went from being a sceptical child specialist to a serene and open-minded person not afraid of death and the future after death. Dr Morse's book includes many stories of young children who were in hospital and 'died' for a moment. Here are some of their experiences:

'Everything went dark when I died, just as I thought it would. Then suddenly my world was filled with light.' One young boy explains vividly how he left his body when his heart stopped. He gives very detailed information that was later agreed to be entirely accurate, including conversations that the doctors had had about him, the way that he was treated, even the way his clothes were cut open. He claims that he was on the ceiling of the operating room looking down on what happened.

Another young girl of eight, Michelle, nearly died in a diabetic coma. She left her body and described in detail what was happening. She saw people that she called doctors who asked her to push a button which would either take her back to her body or she would go with them. What happened to Michelle afterwards is of special interest. She, like many of the other children who have experienced a near death experience, now has a very calm approach to life, and no fear of death. She has become a vegetarian and believes in some kind of God.

Sometimes people are so sad and hurt about the world that they try to commit suicide. Such attempts to die very rarely work; often the person is really crying out for help and understanding. Sometimes the person does come close to death and the experience leads them to a greater understanding of themselves and why they wanted to commit suicide. One story tells of how a young girl, abused and beaten by her parents, decided to kill herself but just at the point when she met with death a spirit being completely covered by a bright white light came to her and said, 'You have made a mistake. Your life is not yours to take. You must go back.' She argued with the being to stay and asked why she should stay, as no one cared. The reply was, 'You're right, no one cares about you, it is your job to care for yourself.' This experience dramatically changed the young girl. She has grown up with a good perspective on life and is living happily with her own children.

In 1986 a school in Wyoming, USA was attacked by a terrorist, who detonated a bomb that should have killed or harmed the 156 children he held hostage. But none of the children was harmed when the bomb went off. They claim that people dressed in dazzling white with bright white heads, like light bulbs, told them to go to the safest place just before the bomb went off. Some of the children describe a voice and some the people, but what is sure is that these children escaped death with the help of their spirit friends.

■ *What you can do*

A near death experience isn't something that you want to experiment with! These are special experiences that happen perhaps all too rarely. You can read about them, though, and be prepared to be open-minded and sympathetic to anyone you meet who claims to have had such an experience. The best book on the subject by far is Dr Melvyn Morse's *Closer to the Light* (Souvenir, 1991). Other books you could read are *Life after Life*, by Raymond Moody (Corgi, 1976), and *Whole in One*, by David Lorimer (Arkana, 1990).

See also OUT-OF-BODY EXPERIENCES, DEATH.

Contact the International Association for Near Death Studies (see ADDRESSES TO CONTACT).

New Age

The New Age is called so because we are already entering an astrological period known as the Age of Aquarius. This New Age brings with it a shift in consciousness, a deeper understanding of ourselves and our place here on earth and in the universe and the signs are everywhere.

The New Age of consciousness recognises that all matter, even people, are composed of energy, described by William Bloom as 'dancing waves of energy, and every particle and movement of the cosmos is related to every other'. Science is beginning to understand this at the same time as we can begin to grasp its complexity with our minds.

This New Age is also teaching us things that we have learned before and need to remember, that our bodies are connected and that we can heal ourselves by diagnosing our whole self, including our emotions and physical body, together as one.

The changing consciousness that we as a human race and planet are experiencing is more than the young travellers living in caravans, it is more than the pagan religions and their revivals, somehow it transcends above all this and is showing us the power of unconditional love. To live in this New Age is to live magically, to be connected to all and to be conscious of all. This might sound like fairytale rubbish to some but it is clear that there are others – perhaps you are reading this right now – who are remembering. Have you ever felt that you have heard this before? For many people in the spiritual world the young people being born today are the stars of creation that will challenge the old system and help us in the transition to new. Are you one of those people?

Every culture looks towards the future, and assesses its past, we are doing no more and no less.

■ *What you can do*

Get past your prejudices about the New Age and start to search for it yourself, within yourself. This book should only be a beginning.

For an all round introduction to New Age ideas try *The Seekers Guide* by William Bloom and John Button (Aquarian, 1993).

Challenge those who accuse you of buying from a 'psychic and spiritual supermarket', your choice is yours and the time to expand your consciousness is now. Challenge the idea of esoteric arts, the time is ready for all of us to learn, not in secretive sects, but openly.

Be aware and conscious of your role here on this beautiful planet. Learn to grow in your mind and in your actions.

Numerology

Numerology is the science of numbers and mathematical laws. The ancient Greeks, Egyptians and Chinese all used numbers to tell the future and to understand systems in the universe and in nature. Pythagoras, the Greek mathematician, said that 'numbers are the first things of nature', and believed that all natural events had some mathematical significance. How otherwise could the astronomer predict when the sun will eclipse or the comet come close to earth?

One of the oldest recorded uses of numerology in divination can be found in the *I Ching* (the Book of Changes: see I CHING). In the *I Ching* the Chinese gave earthly qualities to the even numbers and spiritual or heavenly qualities to the odd numbers. Numbers have been used in Muslim and Hindu temples to create patterns and images of deities. In Noisy-sur-Ecole in France, a prehistoric cave contains one of the first representations of numbers relating to time in the tiny markings in the rock.

Numbers are also associated with days of the week, planets and colours. Our modern-day Monday, Tuesday and so on have more to do with Hindu astrology and numerology than you might think. Look at how the days match up to the planets:

1. Sun (Sunday): Unity; divine purpose; the beginning of all things.
2. Moon (Monday): Duality – black and white, good/bad, dilemma and choice; equality; justice; diversity.
3. Mars (Tuesday): The three principles/ the triangle: earth, mind, universe; personal creativity; thought, word and action; the religious trinities: God the Father, Son and Holy Ghost; Brahma, Vishnu and Shiva.
4. Mercury (Wednesday): The four elements: earth, air, fire and water; the ancient symbol of truth; the four seasons; the four directions; the artistic square (2×2).
5. Jupiter (Thursday): Health and body; five senses; five toes; five fingers; five religious duties of Mohammed: prayer, fasting, purification, alms and pilgrimage to Mecca.
6. Venus (Friday): Intellect and creativity; perfection: sacred Jewish number (the world created in six days); double triangle; crystals found in sixes; Beauty.
7. Saturn (Saturday): Time; good fortune; seven colours in the rainbow; days of the week; deadly sins; scales of music; seven heavens and seven hells; day of rest for Christians, holy day; wisdom; evolution.
8. North Lunar Node of Moon: Balance; first number that can be made into a cube; infinity: beyond time (7); good and bad; night and day.

9. South Lunar Node: Physical (123), intellectual (456) and spiritual (789); last number before unity (10); truth; Neptune; nine months before birth.

All calculations in numerology can be reduced to only nine numbers (zero is not a number). In numerology you reduce everything of significance to a number. So, if you want to know more about yourself, look at your date of birth, the number relating to your surname and your commonly used Christian (first) name. The letters in the alphabet correspond to numbers based on a system devised by the Qabalah and Pythagoras.

1	2	3	4	5	6	7	8	9
A	B	C	D	E	F	G	H	I
J	K	L	M	N	O	P	Q	R
S	T	U	V	W	X	Y	Z	

The name number shows how you will react in various circumstances. So, if your name is Sara it would be represented as $1+1+9+1=12=1+2=3$. Then work out your surname and add the two numbers together to find your name number.

The date of birth represents the way the enquirer sees herself. This is the number corresponding to the day, for example Sunday.

The psychic number is obtained by adding together all the numbers involved in the date of birth: for example 9 November $1961 = 9+1+1+1+9+6+1=2+8=10$

What does it all mean, anyway? There are various different meanings for the numbers. See if you can recognise yourself from the following list.

Qualities and characteristics

1. Personal awareness of characters and ability; ambitious; leadership potential; single-minded, intolerant, stubborn.
2. Personal awareness of feelings and emotions; intuitive; soft, gentle, harmonious, sociable, highly emotional, tending to avoid responsibility.

3. Creativity; brilliant, impatient, adventurous, out of control, rash, brave.
4. Concrete, logical, aware; intellectual, masculine, honest, clumsy, dull, narrow-minded.
5. Aware; healthy, courageous, sympathetic, irresponsible, unreliable.
6. Idealistic, charitable; responsible, trusting, friendly, attractive, soft, unpractical, submissive.
7. Wise, philosophical; deep, comtemplative, morbid, unsociable, slow, psychic.
8. Practical; businesslike, decisive, successful, controlling, blunt, dominant, extremist.
9. Intelligent and determined; tempered, brilliant, understanding, impulsive, lethargic, lacking in concentration.

■ *What you can do*

Work out your own personal numbers from the guides given above and compare the qualities and characteristics with those shown. How can you see yourself in these characteristics? Real numerology is more complicated than this, so do prepare your own research before you read other people's numbers.

Look for other ways that numbers fit into science and religion (the Bible, for instance, has seven angels, four horsemen of the Apocalypse, four apostles and so on).

There are plenty of numerology books worth reading, including *What Number Are You? Your Numbers and Your Life*, by Lilla Bek and Robert Holden (Aquarian, 1992).

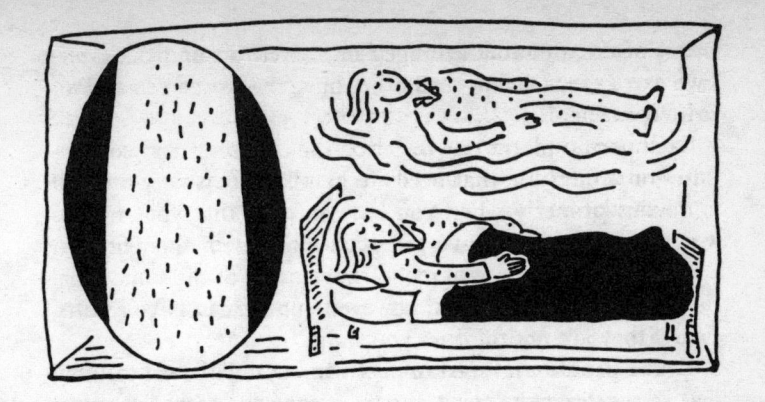

Occult

The word 'occult' comes from the Latin *occultare*, 'to hide', and it is generally used to denote the secret tradition of mystical and magical knowledge handed down through generations. Occult knowledge includes spiritualism, alchemy, magic, and similar esoteric knowledge.

Ouija Board

This is probably one of the first occult objects that will be used by a teenager.

The first recorded use of what later became known as the Ouija board was in AD 371 in the time of the Roman Emperor Valens. A group of enquiring supporters constructed a table made from laurel wood and put a round metal plate on it with the Greek alphabet circling the edge of the plate. A ring was suspended on a piece of thread and after invocations to the gods the questioners asked who would succeed Valens. The ring spelled out the letters THEO. This was the unfortunate name of one of the emperor's administrators, and he was hanged for conspiracy along with the enquirers. But fate and the gods got the last laugh, because when Valens was killed by the Goths in AD 387 he was succeeded by Theodosius.

The Ouija board of today is used in the same way as a pendulum might be used for divination, with the difference that a group of people can use it together. It usually consists of an upturned glass or container with cards showing the letters of the alphabet arranged in a circle around the table. Two extra cards facing each other have the words YES and NO written on them.

Each person places one finger on the container and concentrates on a question that needs to be asked. It is very difficult to do this properly when you have to trust that your friends won't 'accidentally' move the glass along with their fingers, and it's also difficult to agree to concentrate at the same time! But this form of divination, however clumsy, can have results, even if they are not the ones you want.

Young people who start to play with a Ouija board can find that they attract the spirit energy of someone rather nasty. It is not a particularly accurate or empowering form of divination.

■ *What you can do*

There are far more effective and safe ways of divination (seeing into the future) which don't involve asking spirits who might just be hanging about looking for unsuspecting prey. I would err on the side of caution and leave Ouija boards alone. If you must do it, the least you can do is ask for only good spirits to help you find the answers. Ask out loud, and ask your guides to protect you. Imagine a circle of white light surrounding you and the group you are in. Always follow the basic laws of magic: create magic from a desire to love and create happiness; never harm another human being; never misuse magic.

See MAGIC, PROTECTION.

Out-of-body Experiences

It is estimated that between 10 and 20 per cent of the public have at one time or another experienced an OBE, or out-of-body experience. Commonly the person describes sensations where they seem to lift upwards and they can look down on their body from six or ten feet in the air.

Some very famous people have described their out-of-body experiences: Emily Brontë, Goethe, D. H. Lawrence, Charles Lindbergh and Ernest Hemingway. This is what Hemingway wrote: 'I felt myself rush bodily out of myself and out and out and out and all the time bodily in the wind. I went out swiftly, all of myself, and I knew I was dead and that it had all been a mistake to think that you just died. Then I floated, and instead of going on I felt myself slide back. I breathed and I was back.'

In an OBE the astral body – the part of the spirit or soul that continues to live but is an exact replica of our physical body – leaves the physical body for a short time but is usually connected to the physical body by a thread or connecting cord, like a spiritual umbilical cord.

There are certain conditions that increase the chance of having an OBE: sleep and near-sleep, fatigue, meditation, physical and psychological stress, near death situations like accidents, being in hospital with a very serious illness, and even some drugs.

OBEs have been reported in every culture, in every era throughout the world. They are recorded in the Bible, in paintings by Native North American Indians, by the Innuit people, by the ancient Egyptians (who incidentally called the astral or spirit body *ba*). They are so widely reported that sceptics who dismiss one particular story are always perplexed by thousands more of these strange experiences.

Scientists investigating the phenomenon have found that the body experiences a total loss of electrical activity in the physical body, a decrease in rapid eye movements (REM) which usually characterise the state of dreaming and the sort of decrease in brain activity associated with a state of deep hypnosis.

In one famous case, the Reverend Cora L. V. Richmond had a severe and prolonged illness during the late nineteenth century. She described journeys of amazement, in which she visited spirit guides, angels and others who existed in beautiful surroundings where they taught and helped other spirits and human beings towards more evolved states of being and awareness.

One of the most famous out-of-body experiences of recent years is that of Shirley MacLaine, the actress. On a trip to Peru she was meditating and felt her spirit rise above her physical form, held to it by a silver cord. She describes herself feeling limitless, totally elastic, and as she flew even higher she could see the globe of the earth down below. Since that experience she has developed her psychic and spiritual life to such an extent that she has written many interesting books explaining spirituality to others.

■ What you can do

Have you experienced an OBE? Would you know the difference between this and a good dream? An OBE is often the same as astral travelling. (See ASTRAL TRAVELLING.)

Read *Out on a Limb*, by Shirley MacLaine (Bantam Books, 1983), and *Out of Body Experiences*, by Janet Lee Mitchell (Turnstone, 1985).

Paganism

Paganism is an ancient spiritually based religion sometimes known as witchcraft. Pagans perceive God in both male and female forms. They follow earth mysteries and their religion is based on an understanding of the energies of the earth. Latin *pagani* means country dwellers and it is likely that these people were originally farmers and country people who were in tune with the earth they worked on in order to grow food. People who practise druidism and shamanism are also commonly known as pagans.

The Christian hostility to pagans can be seen by the current use of the word 'pagan' to mean someone who doesn't believe in the Christian God. Christians were so afraid of this earth-based religion that they actually took over many of the festivals, holy places, rituals and practices of the religion in order both to entice people away from paganism and towards Christianity and to improve their standing in the local community. Pope Gregory the Great (540–604 AD) ordered that Christian relics be placed in the pagan shrines and gradually converted people to the idea that their deities were either saints (as used in the Christian language) or devils.

Pagans celebrate eight main seasonal festivals. These are positive, happy and energy-giving festivals dedicated to bringing about an inner harmony with the earth.

The Christian Church originally had no holidays of its own and simply 'borrowed' existing ones from the pagans, including Easter, previously dedicated to Eostre, the goddess of fertility (hence the widespread use of Easter eggs as a symbol of fertility).

When it became clear that pagans would not necessarily allow all their festivals and sacred places to be taken over for this 'new religion', mass witch burnings began (see WITCHES AND WITCHCRAFT). It is a tragic conspiracy that churches, governments and educationalists still carry on the myth that pagans are unbelievers and witches are devil worshippers.

Modern pagans, who include druids and witches, have no established church. You can get in touch with individual pagans, but the emphasis is really on networking within a religion of self-awareness and joy. Paganism is one of the fastest-growing religions in Britain today.

■ *What you can do*

Ancient laws still enforced in Britain mean that you are not allowed to join a pagan group unless you are 18 or over, but you can do some studying before that. Learn to challenge the conventional view of paganism. Read all you can about this earth religion that pre-dates Christianity. See EARTH MAGIC.

The following groups can provide information: the Pagan Federation; the Wicca Study Group (runs courses); and the Temple ov Psychic Youth. PaganLink puts pagans in touch with one another and with local pagan groups. (See ADDRESSES TO CONTACT.)

Read *A Witch Alone*, by Marian Green (Aquarian, 1991); *Pagan Celtic Britain*, by Anne Ross (Constable, 1992); *The Pagan Religions of the Ancient British Isles*, by Ronald Hutton (Basil Blackwell, 1991); and *Practical Celtic Magic*, by Murry Hope (Aquarian, 1987).

Palmistry

Palmistry is the art of reading the hands and the lines and markings on the hands. Palmistry is more than a simple form of divination, or fortune-telling; the lines and hand hold many clues to future, past and present health and happiness.

Palmistry is a system of diviation which includes observance, intuition and clairvoyance. The markings and shapes of the hand need to be looked at carefully, both as a whole and in fine detail in order to draw specific and specialised information for the enquirer. The most famous of all palmists must be Cheiro, an Irish occult specialist, christened Louis Hammon in 1866. Cheiro was convinced that even in the Bible knowledge of the use of palmistry and the individual lines of the hand was accepted. He quotes the original Hebrew Book of Job (37:7) 'He [God] sealeth up the hand of every man; that all men may know his work'.

Some evidence exists that many famous men and women throughout the ages have used palmistry to acquire information and power; these include Aristotle, Paracelsus, Alexander the Great, Honoré de Balzac and Alexandre Dumas.

Modern palmists have tried to place palmistry on a scientific basis, looking at how stress, health, the weather, emotions and other factors can influence and change the tiny lines and rings around the fingers and on the palm of the hand. There are literally hundreds of lines, boxes, marks, whorls, loops and other considerations to be taken into account in palmistry. There are too many to list here, so consult a good book for more details.

The police forces of every major country in the world use basic palmistry known as fingerprinting and reading the lines on the fingers to identify criminals, such is the accuracy and uniqueness of the markings on all of our hands.

Many people have a deep desire to find out if their bodies hold any clues to the meaning of their lives. Far from telling them the future, good palmists can usually only tell the past and the future-that-could-be. This point is important: if you believe that fate is already mapped out in your hand then you don't believe you have free will to create your own future. If you could see that events you may encounter in your future can be changed by using knowledge from divination systems like palmistry, you might well take action.

To be really proficient you must give the subject as much time as you can, and, like tarot or other forms of divination, good palmistry is 50 per cent clairvoyance and 50 per cent line-reading.

■ *What you can do*

Start to look at hands everywhere. Notice the shape, size, texture, colour, nails; look at everything, even the dirt under the fingernails. It is possible to tell a huge amount about a person just with this information, before you start to look at the lines and skin ridges found on the inner palm. Ask questions as you look, learn by assessing the person's hand and the answers they give. Could you tell if someone were an office worker? a gardener? a person who is meticulous? a lazy or messy person? someone in bad health?

In order to start learning and interpreting the basic line system on the inner palm it is best to use a teach-yourself book. Cheiro's *Palmistry for All* is the best, but difficult to find in Britain. Try David Brandon Jones's *Practical Palmistry* (CRCS Publications, 1981). This author has his own interpretation of palmistry and its practice. You could also read Rodney Davies's *Fortune Telling by Palmistry* (Aquarian 1987).

At the same time you should be developing yourself in order to be clear about the message you give out when reading palms, just as in reading tarot or any other form of divination. Don't tell people they should be doing this or that. You can only suggest possible futures for them; they have free will and other choices to the ones you suggest. You have a responsibility to be clear about your message and how you put it across.

Don't invent: there is a vast difference between using intuition and making it up as you go along. When you start to read palms, try to learn one or two lines, look at the overall hand and talk only about what you know. See if what you have learnt fits in with what the hand is showing you.

Parapsychology

Since the 1930s studying extrasensory perception has gradually become intellectually acceptable, and at least one university (in Edinburgh) offers a Doctorate in Parapsychology. Studies have shown that at least 50 per cent of the British population have experienced psychic or Psi phenomena; many people look for schools and workshops to guide them and help them to understand what is happening to them.

In the 1950s J. B. Rhine established the first scientifically acceptable method of studying Psi, and named it parapsychology. His work included evaluating psychic volunteers and weighing the statistically normal chances, or probability, that they would have an experience against what was actually happening. His experiments have since been duplicated all over the world.

■ *What you can do*

Contact the Society for Psychical Research and the College of Psychic Studies for lectures and courses (see ADDRESSES TO CONTACT); the Koestler Chair in Parapsychology, Psychology Dept, Edinburgh University, 7 George Square, Edinburgh, EH8 9JZ and the Psi Research Centre.

See PSYCHIC.

Past Lives

If you believe in reincarnation then you must, by definition, believe in past lives. Of course, people who have come on to the earth as new souls will have no history or recollection themselves of their past lives. For many people who are living as educated or spiritually aware souls, however, there is every chance that they have lived before.

Looking back at what you were before is of little help from a psychic perspective unless you wish to use such knowledge to help you psychologically, for instance to overcome phobias or recurring and strange illness. A renowned healer came across a scar on patient's back which had given the man incredible pain and yet there seemed to be no logical medical reason for it. Certainly the patient had not had an accident in this life. On meditation and deep reflection both the healer and the patient came to the conclusion that the wound was from a previous life, and that it hadn't healed properly. With this knowledge the healer was able to begin a process of healing that went beyond the physical and into the aura and psychic energy of the man to enable him to be healed from within. The healing worked.

It is possible to visit past-life therapists who can tell you that you once were an Indian chief or an Egyptian slave but, as in other forms of divination, you get the best results from reputable and careful people.

■ *What you can do*

Be careful. Do you need to know about your previous lives? Aren't you already the sum total of your past right now? Would finding out that you were a princess or a pauper change you? How much of this would be your personal projections and fantasies of your perfect past life?

In accepting the value of reincarnation and the cycles of death and life you might have to face the fact that going back into the past will only be as fruitful as going into the future. In the metaphysics of the New Age the issue is one of free will and the ability to change time and your personal history – including that of the past – so does it really matter what you were?

In *The Truth Vibrations* (Aquarian, 1992) David Icke sets out his personal story. With the help of a medium he has travelled around the world, literally apologising for all the past-life mistakes that he has made. Few of us really need to do this. We could be more accepting and ready to live in the present rather than the past.

See also KARMA, REINCARNATION, HIGHER SELF, NEAR DEATH EXPERIENCES, PERSONAL GROWTH, HEALING, AURA.

Pendulum Power

Pendulums are usually heavy objects held up by a piece of string about 20 cm in length. They are used to find energies underground, places on maps, and objects that you have lost. They are even used to determine the sex of pregnant women's babies when they are still in the womb.

The main reason why a pendulum is heavy is so that it won't blow away in the wind, but if you are thinking of working inside you can use almost any object from a bead to a crystal, a large coin or a ring.

One idea for using a pendulum is to gain insight and answers to questions. The easiest way to do this is to ask 'yes or no' questions. Hold the pendulum in your hand with your index finger pointing down towards the object. Feel the pendulum swing in your hand and gradually give it more and more length until you can sense that it is swinging of its own accord. Start to experiment until you feel comfortable using the device. First of all, use the pendulum over things you know the answers to. For example, ask it 'Do I like coffee?' or 'Is this flower red?'. Hold the pendulum over a cup of coffee or over a flower and watch the result. Of course you will already know if you like coffee or if the flower is red, and thus you can test the pendulum's accuracy by using questions such as these.

The pendulum has basically four moves – it can go from side to side, up and down, round anticlockwise, and round clockwise. It can also be neutral, that is, not moving. Ask the pendulum questions that it can answer in order to help you gain insight into how the energies are detected before you try to locate a long-lost relative using a world map!

If you find you can use a pendulum to great effect you might consider a career in it. According to Colin Wilson, noted psychics like Uri Geller use pendulums to dowse for oil and minerals with maps, and are paid when they locate goods, often ending up millionaires! One typical account of the uses of pendulums is the story of Edgar Devaux, who traced a missing woman to the exact point where she had drowned in Switzerland in 1960.

■ *What you can do*

Make your own pendulum with a length of string or thread and an object that feels appropriate. Practise dowsing until you find your own rhythm and until the yes/no answers are consistent and easy.

Get a friend to fill two glasses with water and to put salt in one of them. Use your pendulum to detect the one containing salt. Ask: 'Does this cup contain salt?'

Try finding electricity cables, water pipes or buried objects. Try looking for your home on a map of your city or town. Don't ask silly questions that the pendulum can't possibly answer like, 'What should I do about it?' Or, 'Should I go left or right?', as you will probably get frustrated and pack the whole thing in. If you are not sure of the validity of your question write it down first; this will also help you to clarify your interest in the answer. Make sure you can answer the question with a 'yes' or 'no' – and have fun.

Read Tom Graves's *The Diviner's Handbook* (Element, 1988); *Pendulum Power*, by Greg Nielsen and Joseph Polansky (Aquarian, 1986), and see DOWSING.

Personal Growth

Growing up isn't just about trying on bigger clothes, going out with boyfriends or girlfriends and getting a job. Personal growth is about the inside of yourself, your mind and your fears growing, changing and developing. Schools rarely teach a young person how to explore the mind just as they rarely teach you about such important experiences as falling in love.

Developing your inner self, your conscious self, is crucial when you decide that you want to live your life magically. Although your experiences of the world may be fewer because you are younger there is no reason why young people shouldn't explore their minds and their soul.

Taking steps towards being a conscious human being will ensure that you become a person with confidence and high self-esteem as well as having a maturing thought process, and a developing psychic and spiritual life.

Personal growth can be developed by a number of means, including meditation, counselling, workshops, psychic awareness, visualisation, joining a spiritual group or religion, a crisis such as a death in the family, inspiration from a book you have been reading and many other means. Not all people will do all these things and it is unlikely that you would find everything from just one of the above. The development of your self will come about by your openness inside yourself: how you think about things, what you do about it, how you carry on relationships with people around you.

Information is important and you should be prepared to believe or disbelieve what you feel. Just because a book says so, doesn't mean you have to do it! Join groups and explore with people you trust and with whom you feel good, not people who are in it for the money or power (see GURUS).

So, what does personal growth look like?

- being aware and awake to your own life;
- listening to your inner voice, or higher self;
- learning to relax and release negative thoughts;
- being conscious and aware of the planet;
- looking after your physical body, including eating good food;
- listening and being prepared to learn from others;
- feeling positive and alive.

■ *What you can do*

Read, read, read! There are literally thousands of books which will give you insights into your inner and outer world. Read as much as you can about alternative ways of thinking, metaphysics, ghosts, your mind, angels, meditation – anything to broaden your horizon and your mind.

Observe. Watch other people and learn from them. We often forget that many of the people around us reflect different parts of our personality.

Take workshops, go to meditation classes, get out there and do positive things to help you along the way. Local libraries, health food shops and alternative magazines usually have listings of courses and workshops. Follow the golden rules: always be responsible for your own body – never let anyone force you to do anything that makes you feel bad or ill, that is frightening to you or against your principles. You don't have to do anything, and you must trust yourself and your inner voice first, not other people.

Listen to yourself whenever you can. Do you carry around old grudges and baggage from experiences that happened years ago? Do you give people positive or negative feedback about themselves? Are your opinions based on prejudice? Or are they carefully worded, loving and inspiring?

Enjoy it. So many people in the New Age movement think that it's all hard work – well it does not have to be. Enjoy and savour your lessons, however hard.

Read *Living Magically*, by Gill Edwards (Piatkus, 1991) and

The Practice of Personal Transformation: A Workbook for Inner Growth, by Strephon Kaplan Williams (Aquarian, 1986).

Poltergeists

When the now famous healer, Mathew Manning, was only eleven, he started to be surrounded by evidence of strange and psychic activity in the form of strange knocking noises, sudden temperature changes in his house, and small fires, messages and levitating furniture. His parents understandably were upset and disturbed by these incidents. They called a psychic researcher, Dr George Owen, from Cambridge University to help them and it took many years to stop the activity surrounding Mathew Manning's psychic energies which had enticed such poltergeist activity.

The word 'poltergeist' comes from the German for 'noisy spirit', and poltergeist activity is generally found around sensitive or highly strung young children during puberty. One description of poltergeist activity describes it as a spoilt, childish, psychic tantrum. This would explain some of the obviously childish activities of the poltergeists like burnings and motiveless destruction of objects in houses. Poltergeist activity rarely actually hurts its victims; the poltergeist prefers to play mischievous and often frightening games with them.

The writer and occult specialist Guy Playfair once described the poltergeist to Colin Wilson as a football of energy that was picked up and 'used', often for mischievous purposes by spirits who were not very intelligent. The energy was most likely to have been provided by a younger member of the family, someone with repressed feelings, with latent sexual desires for instance, or a young person coming into puberty. All these people seem to have an energy around them that attracts these naughty spirits. The spirits will often get bored and leave of their own accord but sometimes they become dangerous, and the line between playful fun and serious interference is pretty thin.

The case of the young Diane Pritchard in Pontefract, recounted by Colin Wilson, is a good example of poltergeist activity. In 1966 the activity started with pools of water on the floor in the kitchen. Water officials couldn't find a leak and when the tap started to spew forth green foam they thought they were in the middle of an American horror movie. Both her brother Phillip and Diane were the source of the energy that had started an amazing course of events that would leave Diane unharmed but the rest of the family shaken. The family started to 'see' the joker, who turned out to be a local monk who had died and had obviously had a bad time. He used Diane's energy to carry out his haunting. One evening he tried to drag Diane upstairs and strangle her. Although there was no proof, she did have red fingermarks around her neck. Mostly the monk played powerful but harmless practical jokes, including moving furniture around, emptying cupboards of teasets and similar pranks.

There are hundreds of stories of poltergeist activity from all over the world. Some are found to be tricks played by silly children, but many cannot be disputed as cases of genuine hauntings, mixing human energy and that of discarnate entities. But though there are genuine cases, they are rare. A poltergeist needs the existence of certain circumstances in the first place. According to Hernani Andrade of Brazil: 'to produce a successful poltergeist all you need is a group of bad spirits to do your work for you for a suitable reward and a susceptible victim who is insufficiently developed spiritually to be able to resist.'

■ *What you can do*

If you suspect you are around poltergeist activity there are things you can do. First check carefully that the activities are not produced by friends or relatives. Ask your spirit guides to help you. If the spirit could be termed a ghost, living on the earth plane but dead, it may not want to admit it is dead and move on to the other side, or spirit world. If this is the case then you can do something yourself but you are probably better off with the help of a medium. Exorcism is not appropriate here, as the poltergeist is likely to be playful and mixed up rather than evil. Ask your guides to tell the poltergeist spirit to go to the other side to see his or her friends, where they will be happy and welcome. Tell this to the spirit yourself whenever you can. Protect yourself with a white light around you and be careful not to get yourself into situations beyond your control. There are mediums who specialise in such activities: call the College of Psychic Studies (see ADDRESSES TO CONTACT) as a starting point.

Read Colin Wilson's *Beyond the Occult* (Corgi, 1988) and *The Link: The Extraordinary Gifts of a Teenage Psychic* by Matthew Manning (Smythe, 1974). Look for similarities in cases that you have heard of. Are there young people around with untapped energy?

Read *A Handbook of Psychic Protection*, by Draja Mickaharic (Rider, 1993), *Psychic Self-Defense and Well-Being*, by Melita Denning and Osborne Phillips (Llewellyn, 1993) and *Psychic Self-Defence* by Dion Fortune (Aquarian, 1988).

Protection

Anyone involved in spiritual or psychic work on any level should be ready to use psychic protection. The main reason why young people get into so much trouble with Ouija boards and similar psychic tools is that they are not protected and have no real idea of the various energies and levels of spirits that they are calling on. It is imperative that you are protected whenever you work, whenever you heal and especially when you work with other people.

Protection takes many forms. The most important and the simplest is protection of the aura. In any kind of psychic attack a certain amount of psychological interference takes place as the attack comes through the aura and into the chakras in order to either control or demobilise the victim. Dion Fortune explains this best:

> until the aura is pierced there can be no entrance to the soul, and the aura is always pierced from within by the response of fear or desire going out towards the attacking entity. If we can inhibit that instinctive emotional reaction, the edge of the aura will remain impenetrable, and will be as pure a defence against psychic invasion as the healthy and unbroken skin is a defence against bacterial infection.

■ *What you can do*

Stand with your feet placed firmly on the ground. Imagine in your mind's eye that you are covered in a bubble of clear, white light. Check the bubble and make sure it has no holes or leaks in it. You can use any similar type of visualisation that creates the same impression. For extra protection add a bandage which, like that of an Egyptian mummy, is wound completely round the body. This form of protection should be done whenever you think of it, at least once a day. Once practised, it takes only a few moments to breathe and think of the bubble. Another high form of protection is to imagine yourself standing inside a perfect green pyramid or a golden sphere.

More serious protection is used when you work with spirits and spirit guides, for example as a medium or healer, or in similar occult areas. You will, by virtue of this work, open your aura and chakras up to possible interference from outside sources. Ectoplasmic (psychic leftover) energy from deceased bodies can attach itself to your body and use the energy in order to manifest such phenomena as poltergeists. Protection of the aura is therefore important, and you can enhance this when working in the psychic field by the following:

When undertaking any work with spirits or energies from the other worlds always protect first your aura and then the room, house or other place where you are. If you see an entity or spirit ask them specifically if they come in peace. If you are not sure of their answer or have an instinctual feeling that they are not telling the truth then ask the question three times until you are clear and sure of them. Never let a spirit body get into yours. If you want to become a medium, take cautious and careful lessons from experienced practitioners who can support and protect you. Use the cross within the circle (⊕), a universal symbol of protection.

Protect yourself from other people, and from their emotions too. You are not responsible for the way that other people feel. Remember that this also means that you *are* responsible for how you feel. Don't take other people's baggage on board, psychically or emotionally, including that of your family and friends. This does not mean you should ignore people or have no sympathy for them. Evaluate your positive thoughts as you grow and consider the effect that other people can have on your aura and spiritual and emotional body by allowing them to drain you or to use you.

The greatest protection you can have is to live a clear, focused life, without addictions and being emotionally balanced. If you don't allow negative emotions to build up you won't have to deal with them. Be clear about who you are and what you want so that there are few ambiguous spiritual or personal relationships. Practise clarity and self-esteem by attending consciousness-raising groups and taking courses like assertiveness training.

Always ask about protection whenever you intend to take classes or workshops on any subjects involved in spiritual and psychic awareness. Always protect yourself when you are at home doing such work alone.

Contact the College of Psychic Studies if you have difficulties with protection (see the ADDRESSES TO CONTACT).

Read *A Handbook of Psychic Protection: Simple and Effective Ways to Surround Yourself with Good Vibrations*, by Draja Mickaharic (Rider Books, 1993); *Psychic Self-Defence*, by Dion Fortune (Aquarian, 1988); and *Psychic Self-Defence and Well-Being*, by Melita Denning and Osborne Phillips (Llewellyn Books, 1993).

See JESUS.

Psychic

The word 'psychic' means 'of the soul' or 'spiritual' and comes from the Greek word *psychikos*. *Psyche* is the Greek for 'mind' or 'consciousness'. Now the word is used primarily to explain the subconscious mind, and a psychic person is someone who is able to pick up energy from or communicate through the subconscious mind with the worlds beyond the physical world which we can all see.

It is perfectly possible for the vast majority of us to be psychic, as the doors to the other worlds are open to all who look for them. It merely takes training and perseverance to open the doors of soul consciousness.

Claims of psychic abilities by individuals often produce scepticism and ridicule from the scientific and religious communities, yet the vast majority of ordinary people believe strongly in such abilities and phenomena. In fact, many governments including that of the United States, have been funding research programmes into telepathy, UFOs, clairvoyance and other psychic phenomena for many years. Police officers have used mediums to help them track down killers, and church officials sanction and take part in exorcisms.

Psychic phenomena can be divided into two main strands: extrasensory perception (ESP) and extrasensory actions (psychokinesis, or PK). Included in ESP are telepathy, precognition and clairvoyance, all of which include heightened inner senses. Extrasensory actions could include PK, healing and out-of-body experiences.

Psychic energy is generated by everything that is alive. You can pick up psychic energy from stones and crystals as well as humans and animals. Psychic energy is a physical substance that can be seen (to the trained eye), touched, moved and moulded. In order to increase your chances of being psychically aware either in your perception or your actions you can train yourself to understand and feel your own psychic energy and that of others. This has a doubly beneficial effect: it is guaranteed to stimulate your self and your soul so that you can discover more about yourself, and it enhances your connection to your higher self or God within.

This book contains names, stories and explanations of psychic ability from all over the world, in every culture, in every class, since records began. It is mind-boggling that intelligent, powerful people in modern society disregard all this evidence simply because they themselves cannot 'see' or experience such phenomena themselves. Psychic energy is really challenging the perceived 'normality' of society, with its rigid and structured ideas about science and rationality; hence the use of the word 'paranormal' (meaning beyond the normal) to describe psychic phenomena.

Whether these experiences will be explained by science in some future period remains to be seen, but they can no longer be argued to be the work of the Devil or some other evil manifestation.

Imagine for a moment that nearly everyone could see the world in only black and white. If you were one of those 'strange', 'lucky' or 'gifted' people who could see the world in colour, how would you explain the colour red? Or green? Imagine the scepticism and ridicule of those who wanted to stay seeing the world in black and white even though you were to explain that they could train themselves to see this colour. And so it is with our psychic abilities. For those who can see auras, bend spoons, talk openly to spirits, heal sickness with light energy, astrally project their bodies, channel writings and pictures or dream of future events the world is more than the physical, but difficult to explain. Sceptics close their minds to such phenomena without even trying to discover the world as it could be.

As we move quickly into the next century we can no longer ignore the intuitive and psychic part of our selves. To heal and rebalance this planet we need to heal and rebalance ourselves first, our minds, our spirits and our actions.

■ *What you can do*

Hold an open mind; everything is possible.

Practise walking with your soul. Allow yourself the pleasure of finding your own inner voice and your higher self connecting with it. Only you have the answers to the questions you will ask. Become a healthy sceptic, develop an enquiring mind that won't automatically believe everything you are told.

Read everything you can, everywhere! There are many books, pamphlets and magazines that will offer advice and exercises to those interested.

Go on courses and workshops whenever you can. Don't just stick to one thing, even if you like it. Do as much as you can. Good books worth reading and places to go are listed at the back of this book.

Read Edgar Cayce's *On Mysteries of the Mind: the Unlimited Scope of Human Consciousness* (Aquarian, 1990).

Psychokinesis

Psychokinesis (PK) literally means mind over matter. In Greek the word means 'movement produced by the mind'; this is where the word first had its origins. You can, by the power of your conscious or unconscious thought, move or bend objects with your mind without touching them, often having some physical influence which you can see and touch.

Probably the most famous person to practise psychokinesis

in front of millions of people is Uri Geller. In the 1970s Geller astonished the world by showing that he was able to bend spoons, forks and knives by merely thinking about them. He says that he would focus on the object in question and repeat the words, 'bend, bend' to himself slowly and deliberately. Uri Geller says that the source of his remarkable powers seems to be an energy from within himself that he doesn't understand. He feels no direct heat or burning when he thinks of the objects; his theory is that there is some kind of kinetic energy which comes from our brains which can be channelled into objects in order to make them bend.

Not everyone can do this, but many people claim to have the powers of Uri Geller. After his performances were seen by large numbers of people, however, many of those claiming to be 'new Gellers' were exposed or caught cheating. A group of schoolchildren were caught when they underwent tests at the University of Bath. They were not aware that while they were supposedly using the power of their mind, a one-way mirror showed them bending cutlery with their feet and twisting it with both hands.

It is of course possible that people can use their brain power to move or change physical objects outside their body. Psychokinesis researchers suggest that the state of mind is one of the most important reasons for success. In normal day-to-day activity the brain operates on beta waves, when you are alert, awake and moving around. If you are worried or nervous about something your brain could continue to register beta waves even when you are asleep. When you meditate or listen to relaxing music, are hypnotised or watch a boring programme on television, your brain registers alpha waves. It is when your brain registers alpha waves that researchers usually find the best PK effects.

When you are in a state of deep trance, your brain usually registers theta waves, which can help suppress pain in the body. Yogis and fakirs use theta waves successfully so that they can lie on a bed of nails or walk across hot coals. Delta waves are emitted when you sleep and you feel relaxed and comfortable.

One scientist, John Hasted, looked for an answer as to why our minds can move or bend objects without touching them.

In the mid-1970s he conducted a series of experiments with schoolchildren who had all claimed some powers of PK. Hasted always maintained that when his subjects were in a relaxed state of mind he was able to register more dramatic levels of energy and change. His experiments led him to believe that the children gave off some kind of energy that sometimes was twisted, like a cone, or ribbon. This twisting, he suspected, was the cause of the bends and twists in the spoons and keys he had hidden around the rooms the children were tested in. When the children concentrated too hard they made their own lives difficult because they were usually unable to produce the desired effect!

Levitation is also a form of PK. In the early days of mediums and seances, it was thought that objects like chairs and tables that mysteriously 'flew' across the room did so because 'the Devil' was at work or because the dead that they were contacting threw them. These days it is thought much more likely that the force behind such activity is psychokinesis on a larger scale, as a group of people may find themselves in a relaxed state and each may contribute to the energy required.

■ What you can do

Ask yourself if it is very useful or productive to spend time trying to bend a spoon with your mind when your hands will do the job just as well and in a shorter time! However, the roots of PK work in a way that could alter your life, and offer positive benefits.

Through meditation and relaxation we can get our minds to a state where alpha waves are emitted from the brain, and through visualisation we can 'see' ourselves passing exams, or becoming healthy and fit. This apparently will lead us to do the absolutely appropriate thing to help us achieve success, like practising more regularly.

Pain barriers can also be altered. Imagine the change next time you attend the dentist and it doesn't hurt. Prepare yourself by getting into a relaxed state and visualising the end of the session with the dentist or doctor; imagine yourself smiling, without pain. It will help!

See VISUALISATION for more interesting techniques; also MEDITATION.

Psychometry

Psychometry is being sensitive to the psychic energy contained in an object which will often reveal the history or life of that object, including the energy of the people who touch it. According to the psychic teacher William Bloom, psychometry seems to indicate that everything that has ever happened to an object is captured on record and can be released and read like a book whenever you want.

There are many famous cases of psychometry in action; so many, in fact, that it is thought to be one of the easiest forms of psychic experience available.

One case, just after the First World War, was that of a patient Maria Reyes de Zierold who was an insomniac. While she underwent treatment by hypnosis the medics found she had increased psychic powers as well as the ability to 'get inside' the mind of various objects. She was able to tell the astonished doctors where certain objects had originated and who owned them. She could also 'taste and smell' the objects inside her own body without ever touching them.

You can witness some amazing 'party tricks' performed by psychics who can read objects and tell information about and the history of an object that no one else could know, to the surprise and enjoyment of the assembled guests.

■ *What you can do*

Practise psychometry with friends. Get everyone to place an object that is dear to them – a ring, keys, and so on – in a dish or bag and let each person remove someone else's object. Concentrate on this object in a quiet mood for five to ten minutes. Notice any pictures that arise in your mind. Be open to these pictures, and even to other senses that come from these objects. Hold them in one hand and then the other, notice which hand feels easiest. Then tell the group what you can sense and try and identify who the object belongs to.

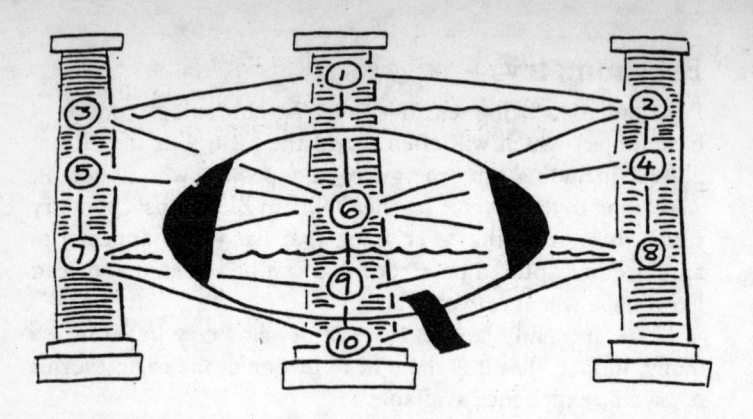

Qabalah

The qabalah is an ancient and immortal spirit of mystical tradition of the interpretation of the Scriptures. According to Hebrew legends, the secrets of the qabalah were passed down from 'mouth to ear' to initiates and students for many centuries.

The qabalah is not a religion, nor a spiritual practice; more a deep and deliberate method of spiritual attainment using symbolism and inner work as its core. The works prepared and passed down by the initiates were not published until the thirteenth century, when a Spanish qabalah specialist wrote the *Zepher ha Zohar*, commonly known as the *Zohar* (splendour). He claimed the work was channelled writing from a rabbi and mystic, Simeon bar Yohai, and the work became the cornerstone of the current qabalah.

Qabalah, kabbālâ and cabbala are all correct spellings depending on whether the Greek, Hebrew or current esoteric use is called for.

The qabalah attempts to present a symbolic and spiritual explanation of the universe and its beginning and end, including our relationship to the Godhead. To do this it creates the 'Tree of Life' in which the ten planes of activity are based. These ten sephiroths, as they are called, are linked to the Tree of Life by 22 paths, corresponding to the 22 letters in the Hebrew alphabet. The sephiroths represent parts of human consciousness, and each one holds the key to and the explanation of all the rest. Each sephiroth has three aspects:

philosophy, psychism and magic. Dion Fortune, who studied the qabalah for many years, wrote that it represented the yoga of the West, and indeed the secret traditions and teachings of the qabalah have been revived by organisations such as the Golden Dawn, the Rosicrucians and Dion Fortune's more recent Fraternity of the Inner Light.

Eliphas Levi was a nineteenth-century occultist who claimed the connection between the qabalah and the tarot pack. Perhaps the 22 major arcana cards of the tarot provide clues to understanding this obscure work. The qabalah has also been linked with alchemy and astrology and it is a source of general esoteric (hidden) information and understanding using both religious and biblical as well as divinatory sources and meditation.

■ *What you can do*

This is a heady, intellectual method of understanding the full manifestations and implications of universal awareness, and long study is required to understand the basics.

The student of qabalah needs to have a serious interest in the esoteric arts, since the teachings are not easy and it may take several years before even an accomplished person fully understands their complexities.

Recommended works include *Practical Guide to the Qabalistic Symbolism*, by Gareth Knight (Kahn & Averill Press, 1990) and Dion Fortune's *The Mystical Qabalah* (1935; reprinted by Aquarian, 1987). Courses are available at the Saros Foundation (see ADDRESSES TO CONTACT).

See also ASTROLOGY, ALCHEMY, TAROT CARDS.

Reincarnation

For tens of thousands of years humans have created rituals and blessings for the dead with the common belief that some part of the dead person lived on, beyond death. Reincarnation is a phenomenon known and elaborately discussed by every major religion throughout time. Even the Christians believed in reincarnation until relatively recently.

Ice Age man and woman were known to put flowers over the bodies of the dead and ancient Egyptians mummified their relatives and left them with as much gold and jewellery as they could afford to help the deceased in the next life. According to the Egyptian Book of the Dead, when a person died some other part of themselves was born and special prayers were said to release the *sahu* or spiritual body, which then travelled to join the *ba* (soul) and then on to heaven.

Buddhism, Hinduism and Sikhism all have reincarnation and the wheel of life, death and rebirth as a central part of their religious beliefs. The Greek Pythagoras brought intellectual discussion about reincarnation to the West about 550 BC and Plato discussed it in even more detail in later years. Reincarnation was also taught as a central subject in the schools of Socrates and Aristotle. At the same time the mystic shamans of central and southern America were also teaching about the great wheel of life. Native North American Indians teach white Westerners the secrets of reincarnation today through their medicine wheels.

The process to eliminate references to reincarnation in

Christianity began with Constantine the Great (AD 274–337) and continued with the Ecumenical Church Council called by the Byzantine Emperor Justinian at Constantinople in AD 553. One of the reasons was to rid the Church of the Gnostic belief in reincarnation and the learning and teaching of Christ Jesus and his psychic powers.

The origins of intellectual thought on reincarnation are impossible to trace, leaving investigators to assume that the idea was common practice because it could be seen and understood by so many. Buddhist belief in karma was directly connected to reincarnation: after all, if you didn't come back after life, then how would you learn all the lessons that you needed to learn in order to ascend into enlightenment? (See KARMA.)

There are many stories of people who claim to have been living in another life before this one and some that have been investigated seem so watertight and the evidence so clear that it would take a seriously sceptical person to dismiss all the stories and all the evidence. One famous case, which is recorded in many places, is that of the young Indian girl Shanti Devi who declared, at the age of four, that she had been married to a cloth merchant called Kedar Nath Chaubey. Her schoolteacher was intrigued and wrote to the address she had given only to be shocked to receive a reply from the man himself. When Shanti was taken from Delhi to Muttra she was able to recognise and name a huge list of relatives and even point out where she had previously hidden money!

From the spirit world perspective one of the most important reasons why spirit beings and teacher guides try to communicate with us is to tell us of reincarnation and life after death. If we fully realise the implications of living again and again we might be more sure, more careful, more spiritual in this life so as to use the experience fully for what we have intended it to be.

In the spirit world we choose all our main experiences and lessons and we also choose our families and the groups of people who will play a major part in our lives and in our understanding of ourselves. These lessons may often be painful, or puzzling, but they will help us to affirm ourselves and help our soul along its path towards its own enlightenment.

Past-life therapy is one way in which it is possible to draw on the experiences of your past life and the lessons which you learned, or didn't learn, and move forward. (See PAST LIVES.)

Reincarnation is like school: you go to each class for a lifetime, learn all sorts of things and go back home for the holidays, agreeing to return for the new life when you have sorted out your curriculum. It is most likely that we have had several hundred lives on this planet already, and as we progress as souls we share and disseminate our knowledge and collective understanding to others along the way. Just because we think of our lessons and experiences before we get here don't make the mistake of thinking that nothing can be changed and that you are left to work only with fate and destiny as your teachers. On this planet we have a magic partner in our destiny – free will. Although we may have agreed with our spirit guides and friends in the other world that the best lesson for our soul would be to learn about, say, a dependency problem like drugs, it is up to us when we are here whether we decide to take the opportunity to do something about it.

■ *What you can do*

Many New Age and spiritual schools of thought believe firmly in reincarnation: it is often a central theme in their view of the reason why we are here on this planet. There's plenty to read about this subject. I recommend *Exploring Reincarnation*, by Hans TenDam (Arkana, 1990); *Understanding Reincarnation*, by J. H. Brennan (Aquarian, 1990) *The Reincarnation Workbook*, by the same author (1990); and Jeffrey Iverson's *More Lives than One?* (Pan Books, 1976).

Discuss the evidence for reincarnation: bring the subject up with your friends and even in religion lessons/discussions. See what comes up for you when you meditate and think deeply about the subject. Read it from the spirit's point of view in 'Coming Home: The Transition Called Death' in the American magazine, *Spirit Speaks*, No.39. (SEE MAGAZINES).

Think carefully about reincarnation. If you are going to come back, what do you think you are here for now? Why would you want to come back? Is it to do something that you could do now? See also DEATH, NEAR DEATH EXPERIENCES, GHOSTS.

Religion and Religious Beliefs

Most societies, whether modern or ancient, have some form of organised religious belief systems that people look to for inspiration and spiritual guidance. As time passes, religions may come and go, often having revivals and quiet times over long periods.

Christianity, Islam, Hinduism, Buddhism, Sikhism and Judaism, like most other major religions, require cultural as well as spiritual acceptance within a community. Most school curricula educate young people in only a few of the main religious ideas, teaching the historical and intellectual basics through books and attention to spiritual practice. Our religious ideas are changing, however, and rapid technological advances coupled with the great numbers of people travelling abroad, especially in the last fifty years, have brought us more in touch with many varied religious groups and spiritual ideas.

Young people are looking for new religious experiences outside those traditionally accepted by their communities and societies. Parents have become afraid that their ideas don't seem to be accepted any longer, and they feel that their children are slipping away from their culture. The shift in consciousness in modern times has meant that many people have given up the ideas of traditional religious organisations. Falling attendance at churches certainly proves that, but there is a new understanding as people look for answers to questions from other routes, especially from within.

Some new religious groups stringently require difficult behaviour, even withdrawal from society. These are more likely to be cults, some of which have been accused of brainwashing young people by using unknown and unusual methods, including psychological pressure, to make them join. It is true that when an individual finds a special part of themselves through religious experience they can often become overjoyed. Life takes on a new meaning and this is often why some things just don't seem to be as important any more, including families and money.

Many cults have been set up in Britain in the last thirty years. One woman who joined a famous cult in the late 1960s told about her experiences. She was 17 at the time, and the cult she joined is still in existence. She remembers being told several times that this organisation had all the answers and that other religions were irrelevant and ignorant. She made friends and felt a strong sense of community with these people, yet felt she was being brainwashed several times but was powerless to move out or do much about it. This woman spent ten years with the group and unfortunately regrets much of that time.

They practised transcendental meditation and offered group philosophy classes which also included group 'sharings' and personal openness. As with most cults, the key things to watch out for are a lack of personal identity, manipulation or coercion into the acceptance of rules and regulations, and a feeling that this group/idea/religion is the only one worth being involved in. There is an uneasy line between a religious group set up on co-operative, unconditional principles which has rules of conduct for its members to follow, and cults that mentally and emotionally manipulate people into carrying out those rules.

Although new religions and spiritual ideas have emerged, most of the widely accepted religions have a few themes in common: the belief that all life is sacred and that we are all connected together, and that God, in any form, shines light and understanding through all our problems and the world. Here are some of the main truths that connect these faiths.

Christianity

'All things whatsoever ye would that men should do to you, do ye even so to them' (Matthew 7:12).

Judaism

'What is hateful to you, do not to your fellow man. That is the law: all the rest is commentary' (Talmud, Shabbat 31a). 'The Lord is my Light, and my salvation; whom then shall I fear?' (Psalms 27:1).

Native American

'Respect for all life is the foundation' (Chief Oren Lyons) 'The Light of Wakan-Tanka is upon my people' (Song of Kablaya).

Islam

'No one of you is a believer until he desires for his brother that which he desires for himself' (Sunnab).

Buddhism

'Hurt not others in ways that you yourself would find hurtful' (Udana-Varqa, 5:18). 'The radiance of Buddha shines ceaselessly'.

Taoism

'Do not unto others what you would not have them do unto you' (Analects 15:23). 'Following the Light, the sage takes care of all' (Lao-Tzu).

Hinduism

'This is the sum of duty: do naught unto others which would cause you pain if done to you' (Mahabharata 5:1517). 'In the effulgent lotus of the heart dwells Brahman, the Light of Lights' (Mundaka Upanishad).

Sikhism

'Don't create enmity with anyone as God is within everyone' (Guru Arjan Devji 259 Guru Granth Sahib). 'God, being Truth, is the one Light of all' (Adi Granth).

The idea of God being within everyone of us is also a truth found in most of the main religions. We are all the sons and daughters of God, and God is within us all. How we choose to use this information and live our lives is up to us as individuals but the strongest faiths are those found within ourselves and those that connect with our own understanding of the place that we have here on this beautiful planet.

■ *What you can do*

Be open to all religions and faiths; they are built on idealism that began with light and a quest for spiritual understanding. Don't get caught up in judgements like, 'My religion is better than your religion.' If God (the Godhead/the Universal Energy/the Divine Creator) is within us all, there is plenty of space for everyone. Imagine that only one type of music was acceptable in the world. How boring our love of music would be! Wars are fought and people are killed because of religious dogma. Even in Europe people in Northern Ireland and in the Czech republic are killed almost daily because of complex religious and territorial battles.

Investigate all the religious experiences you can: ask people in your community and read about these religions.

Be prepared to realise that some of the modern religions have faults as well as good points; become a healthy enquirer. Never believe everything that is said to you about a religion unless you feel it deep within yourself too. Don't join cults, communities and groups without carefully thinking about it. Ask questions, see how openly and honestly the answers are given. Do you feel comfortable with and are you clear about all that is asked of you? Would you become a Roman Catholic nun or Buddhist monk without questions?

See BUDDHISM, DRUIDS, GODS AND GODDESSES, JESUS, PAGANISM, UNCONDITIONAL LOVE, VOODOO, ZEN, NEW AGE, WITCHES AND WITCHCRAFT.

Rituals

A ritual is any organised, specific form of magic, spiritual work, festival or prayer that is done with intent. This means that you think about the elements of spirit, joy or whatever you wish to evoke and you deliberately set out to bring these elements into your life. Even washing in your bath can be a ritual – if you decide that you wish it to be more than a soapy bath it becomes something more.

In the Middle Ages much hysteria was raised by those who believed that women and men who carried out rituals during worship of the earth, sun or moon were devils. Many religions even today carry out rituals which involve sacrifice, such as the Christian use of red wine as a symbol of the blood of Christ and the host (bread) as a symbol of his body. Muslim rituals include fasting for 40 days at Ramadan. Church services and similar religious services and festivals are complex and stylised rituals attended by millions of people throughout the world.

Use candles, purifying water, incense, oils, herbs, flowers, ribbons and fabrics, crystals and stones, present-giving and receiving, as tools to evoke an atmosphere and to create ritual.

Modern rituals can be carried out with intent rather than a notebook of do's and don'ts. You can create your own ritual to request help with passing exams, to send love or healing to a friend or to expand your understanding of a problem. Use tools that you feel comfortable with, like candles and herbs. Check their meaning with your own intuitive feelings and create the right atmosphere for your magical work.

Call upon your guardian angel and your guides to help you whenever necessary.

The more people who carry out rituals together the more potent the energy that can be sent or received.

Read William Bloom's *Sacred Times: A New Approach to Festivals* (Findhorn Press, 1990); *The Women's Spirituality Book*, by Diane Stein (Llewellyn, 1987); *The Crone's Book of Words*, by Valerie Worth (Llewellyn, (1988) and *A Handbook of Psychic Protection*, by Draja Mickaharic (Rider, 1993).

See MAGIC, HIGHER SELF, GUARDIAN ANGELS OR GUIDES, MEDITATION, CANDLES, INCENSE AND OILS, FESTIVALS.

Runes

The word 'rune' derives from the ancient Germanic which means mystery or 'secret that is whispered'. Rune stones have been used as a form of divination from Palaeolithic times and are often said to be the closest form of earth-based or ecological divination. Runes provided ancient Europeans with wisdom and power, and evidence of their existence in 1300 BC has been found in Sweden in the Germanic alphabet in the fifth century BC and as inscriptions on helmets and stones around Europe at the time. Each stone is inscribed with a Germanic letter which has many meanings.

Rune stones are said to bear the letter which holds the key to the answer needed to the enquirer's question. In order to tap into the energy and memory of the stones and their meaning you should meditate and 'tune in' to them. The runes are a gateway for those who have forgotten the reason why the soul decided to come to earth; by using them you are supposed to find the spiritual knowledge that you need to remember your path.

■ *What you can do*

Read *The Runic Workbook* and *Discovering Runes* by Tony Willis (Aquarian, 1986) and *The World Atlas of Divination*, by John Matthews (Eddison Sadd Editions, 1992) for a good historical perspective.

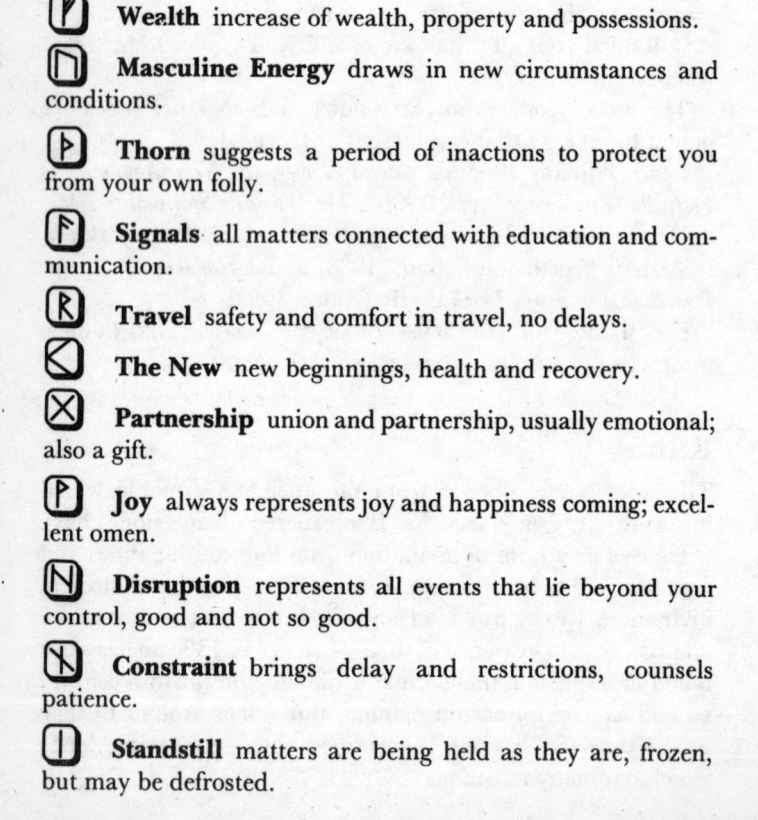

The Runes

Wealth increase of wealth, property and possessions.

Masculine Energy draws in new circumstances and conditions.

Thorn suggests a period of inactions to protect you from your own folly.

Signals all matters connected with education and communication.

Travel safety and comfort in travel, no delays.

The New new beginnings, health and recovery.

Partnership union and partnership, usually emotional; also a gift.

Joy always represents joy and happiness coming; excellent omen.

Disruption represents all events that lie beyond your control, good and not so good.

Constraint brings delay and restrictions, counsels patience.

Standstill matters are being held as they are, frozen, but may be defrosted.

Harvest suggests reaping of rewards for efforts, when the time is right.

Turnaround indicates situation leaping back into life again, and the miraculous transmutation of obstacles into stepping-stones.

Revealing something hidden or secret will come to light; the truth.

Vulnerability the willing sacrifice of lesser good for greater good; protection in new areas of life.

Wholeness assures the successful resolution of problems; health, and physical strength.

Victory victory in any situation with an element of contest or competition.

Birth the physical birth of something; all domestic affairs.

Movement a change for the better; tackling problems in the right spirit.

Mankind rune of interdependence; expect assistance and co-operation.

Conception counsels you to follow your intuition; don't be afraid to go with the flow.

Completion successful endings; end of one phase and expansive beginning of another.

Transformation slow and measured progress which will eventually lead to complete and heartening change, like summer after a long winter.

Possessions the things money can buy, especially home; also inheritance.

The unknowable those elements which are fated and inevitable, and cannot be avoided; karmic law in action.

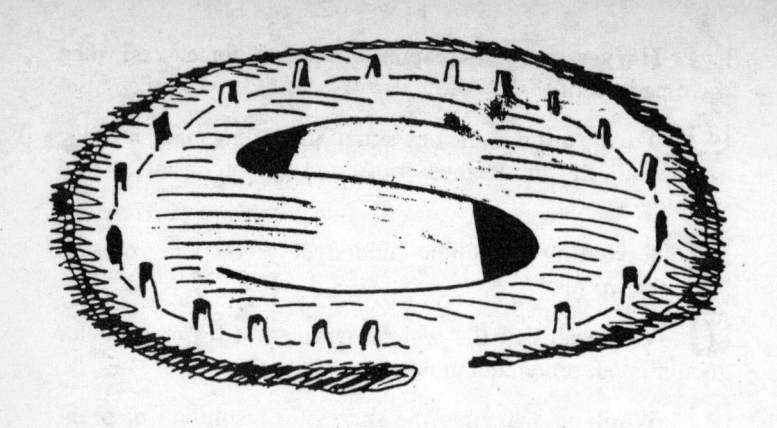

Sacred Stones

The mystery of Stonehenge is still to be deciphered. Work on the gigantic stones probably began about 2500 BC. The largest stones were thought either to have been brought from Wales or Ireland by a glacier 200,000 years beforehand, or somehow to have been carried by Neolithic people. The whole thing probably took about 1,000 years to build and the most reasonable theory put forward for its use is that it was a sacred observatory for the study of the stars and astrology.

A Professor Thom, Chair of Engineering at Oxford University in the 1960s, put forward a scientifically based theory which would support this idea. He claims that the designers would have to have had a working knowledge of the theory of Pythagoras, that Stonehenge was constructed using the help of menhirs (single standing stones as accurate astrological markers) and that the complex knowledge needed to make the stones geometrically and mathematically correct would have had to come from extremely sophisticated and dedicated scholars, well versed in astronomy, architecture and geometry.

Other stone circles have been found across Europe and North Africa and in the USA. Most of the stones are thought to be neolithic, having been constructed during the later part of the Stone Age, but others have been accurately dated right up to the Middle Ages. Some smaller stones have been found to be chambers for burials or ceremonies. Some, like the French stones lining the road at Carnac, were said to have been erected for astronomical reasons. In Madron in Cornwall there is a huge stone called Men an Tol alongside a ring. According to local folklore, people could pass their sick children and relatives through this ring to cure them. The famous stones at Avebury hold a different meaning. They alternate in shape, and form a great wide circle. It is thought that they were representations of male and female fertility and that many rituals took place within the circle.

In Brittany more than 1,000 stones meander in the countryside in lines for nearly a mile. Over many hundreds of years, folklore tells us, local farmers brought sick cattle to the site. Other stones mark the entrance to burial grounds, like the famous Druids' Altar in Ireland.

While the stones are still standing they offer no simple clues to their real identity and purpose; we can only piece together the reasons for their construction and imagine their ancient powers. Many psychics have claimed that there are extraordinary powers found at the sites where these stones have been erected, and either they were built in order to harness the power or they attracted the energy towards them. Most of these constructions were built over 3,000 or 4,000 years ago, but no one can agree exactly how.

The first modern acknowledgement of the connection between the stones and the sun and stars came with Martin Brennan's *The Stars and the Stones*. In this he noticed and marked the alignments of the stones to major festivals like equinoxes, lunar risings and settings. A major work undertaken in 1983 by George Terence Meaden, *The Goddess of the Stones: the Language of the Megaliths*, takes the whole thing one step further, bringing together a mathematical understanding of how the circles were constructed and the important symbolisms of meteorology, archaeology, geometry and religion. His explanations and work are of crucial importance in understanding the religion of the Goddess, dating from Neolithic times. The sacred stones give obvious clues that the peoples of those times must have known a great deal about science.

The stones, burial chambers and similar megaliths are now thought to be connected to this religion of the earth and of the cosmic mother. Circles and spirals, details in their thousands through Europe are recognised as the unending regeneration of the body in cycles of life, death, rebirth. The cycles of the moon and sun would have played an important part in this philosophy and the stones, built to use the maximum energy from such natural forces, were literally 'suntraps' where rituals could take place.

■ *What you can do*

A visit to standing stones is recommended, and there are plenty of books and maps. Why not organise a group? Notice if you sense any extra energies around such stones. Can you imagine how and why they were built?

Read *Mystic Places*, (TimeLife Books, 1987), which has the best full colour plates of the standing stones, *Earth Mysteries*, by Philip Heselton (Element, 1991); and *Points of Cosmic Energy*, by Blanche Merz (C. W. Daniel, 1987). The most important work on the subject is George Terence Meadon's *The Goddess of the Stones* (Souvenir Press, 1991).

Campaign to stop the destruction of any local stones in your area. Recently archaeologists and conservationists have voiced fears as modern farmers simply move stones to get to the land they need, and Ordnance Survey maps leave out stones that they don't understand or that are not big enough to be of importance to them. These are part of our cultural, spiritual heritage and should be preserved and understood.

Sceptics

For every single case of paranormal events there are, of course, the sceptics. These people need to find a scientific way to express or understand exactly how the supernatural event actually worked, and of course they do an important job in exposing tricksters and fraudulent liars. The sceptics reproduce so-called psychic phenomena exactly as the psychic does, often with the same results, but interestingly enough they can never prove 100 per cent that psychic phenomena do not exist.

One solid sceptic, James Randi, a magician himself, has spent much of the last fifteen years trying to undermine and expose what he called the fake tricks of Uri Geller. He claims that the effects that Geller demonstrates to the public are no more than clever stage tricks and that Geller should stop claiming that he is psychic. Randi has been supported by the American Committee for the Scientific Investigation of Claims of the Paranormal and has received funding of at least $270,000 to discredit the work of psychics around the world.

In 1991 Randi made his name in Britain through a series of television programmes in which he set out to expose fake mediums, dowsers, aura readers, etc. He carries around a cheque for $10,000 which he says he will give to anyone who proves their psychic ability to him. His critics say that the conditions he insists on before testing rule out most people anyway, for one reason or another.

It's unfortunate, because he probably could have something interesting to offer the debate, but his personal battle to discredit Uri Geller makes him look like an angry and narrow-minded man instead of a logical thinker who wants to know the answers.

Others have also joined in the debate. The *Skeptic* magazine has a following of nearly 1,000 people in the UK and each issue is devoted to exposing and explaining the trickery and magic of psychics. Dr Donnelly was quoted in Jean Ritchie's *The Unbelievers: Inside the Supernatural* as saying, 'We feel that belief in strange and unproved things is not a good way for a society to progress' and, 'If society in a large way came to depend on divine guidance – consulting palmists, astrologers, mediums and the like every week – we would begin to lose any sense of being responsible for ourselves, we would be putting our destinies in the hands of random factors.'

Sceptics also claim that most of what we think of as supernatural is in fact only random chance. We can have a certain number of exact hits when we guess numbers or when we find something to marvel at; for instance the number of times we will dream about a death in the family is supposedly connected not to the paranormal explanation that we met up with that person in our dreams, or our astral bodies, but that we had a good chance of dreaming about it anyway and it only becomes significant to us when our relatives do actually die.

Another sceptic, Dr Blackmore, says, 'obviously I don't believe in the paranormal, there are lots of phenomena for which at present we don't have full and complete explanations, and so the research must continue. I believe we will find good, mystical, psychological and even physical explanations of everything eventually.'

Experiments and research are taking place, at Edinburgh University for example, but these experiments are grossly underfunded so far. Perhaps ordinary people will come up with the answers just as the scientists have found their own.

■ What you can do

Become a healthy sceptic. Don't believe in what you hear unless it feels right and proper for you. Look at your own personal motivations for wanting to hear whatever has been said or shown to you. Be aware and cautious with mediums who want to take large sums of money and offer you health and happiness; plenty of people have been caught. Don't forget that there are good and bad practitioners of every trade, so look carefully before you accept anyone's advice.

Make sure that you are aware of answers that could apply to just about anyone – don't be conned, for example, when someone tells you, 'You want to be liked and needed by other people.' Well, who wouldn't?

Investigate whenever you think you have had a psychic experience yourself. Make notes and try to replicate the happening. Was it a fluke? Was it chance? Did something really happen or did you just want it to?

Should you want an alternative view, read Jean Ritchie's excellent *The Unbelievers: Inside the Supernatural* (Fontana, 1992) and get hold of a copy of the *Skeptic* magazine (see MAGAZINES).

Scrying

Looking deep into crystals for pictures that tell the future is known as scrying, and the art of scrying has been handed down for thousands of years. Magicians used to follow instructions from Graeco-Egyptian texts, written around AD 100 which had words to summon up spirits and demons in bowls of water, ink or through a crystal ball. Christians and Jews in the Middle Ages often used a mirror to search for lost property, to identify thieves and lawbreakers and to see the future.

The art of scrying angered Pope John XXII around the beginning of the fourteenth century, which is how the occult and divination practices got their bad name. The Pope accused people in his court of working in league with the Devil, and claimed that they summoned up the Devil while scrying. He ordered the destruction of all books that discussed the subject, handwritten and illustrated, and they were burned, lost for ever.

Probably the most famous scryer was Nostradamus. Born in 1503 in France, he was influenced by the Jewish, Roman Catholic and other religions. Egyptian magical folklore suggested that the best way to scry was to stand a bowl of water on a three-legged stool, and this is what Nostradamus did. By the time he was in his 50s he was an accomplished doctor and astrologer, supported by the sympathetic Queen of France, Catherine de Medici, and had written his first major text of predictions.

The work was difficult to read and interpret, since Nostradamus used at least five languages and wrote obscure, poetry-like texts. But they did go down well in public and even today his books can be bought around the world. During the Second World War in Europe passages from the Nostradamus texts were forged and distributed to foretell defeat in order to psychologically undermine the enemy.

Scrying was a crime during the witch-burning times and many women who dared to look into their crystal balls, or in a pond of water, for the answer to their problems were murdered by either the Church or state in a panic-stricken belief that the Devil was being summoned.

Arab scrying is unusual in that oil or black ink is poured into the palm of the hand and the visions are seen through it. Most cultures have used polished glass, crystals or water to see through. It is unlikely that there are any real visions inside the glass or crystal itself but clairvoyants who use this method will tell you that you will be able to concentrate in a clear way on the question by looking into the centre of the empty glass. A sort of trance state will occur, rather like meditation, and spirit guides and angels can be summoned to answer questions. To the uninitiated or unwise, scrying will at the very least represent pictures of the ego, the self and what it expects.

To the practised it could be an amazing door into the unknown and the world of the occult.

■ *What you can do*

Choose your crystal carefully and make sure you feel happy with it; it could be glass or water or even try the Arab way with black ink. You will need to 'look' at the crystal for about 20 minutes each day, to build up a relationship with it and to practise 'seeing'. Get yourself into a meditative atmosphere, making sure that the room is quiet and restful. Clear your mind of thoughts. Eventually you might start to see pictures. Make a good note of what is happening and don't be too quick to jump to conclusions about what the visions mean. It could all too easily be a part of your subconscious mind that you are just getting to understand. Be ready to think long and hard about the meaning, and 'tell' the crystal that you are only willing for important and meaningful visions to show themselves.

Notice how often crystal balls and crystal-gazing comes up in conversation, often as the subject of abuse or belittlement.

Shamanism

Shamans use ancient methods of divination including calling spirit ancestors who can see the strength of the 'current future'. The shamans would interpret natural events like storms and skies and omens like deaths and shamanism is without doubt the earliest known and most far-reaching religion. Shaman rituals are still performed today all over the world. These magical people can go into a trance and 'become' at one with gods and spirit ancestors just as mediums do. In shamanistic ceremonies animals are often used, especially because of the close connection to hunting within the rituals and trances.

The oldest cave painting dated has been found in a French cave called Les Trois-Frères. It is thought to be at least 15,000 years old and shows a shaman hunter disguised as one of the bison that is hunted, right in among the bison, hidden from their view by supernatural phenomena. This theory is again stated by the anthropologist Popov, who recorded trances among the Tungus people of eastern Siberia who could resonate with animal spirits.

In *The spiral dance*, the women's spiritual writer Starhawk describes how the bison dance and dance with the shamans until the bison fall into a frenzy of trance and run over a cliff to their death. This is one of the ways in which tribes supposedly killed such animals for food. The shaman's role in the community was to journey beyond physical reality and into the worlds of the unknown to reveal the future. These revelations would come through dreams, through trances moved into by drumming and musical rhythms, through 'discussions' with their magical animal guides and friends and from natural events.

Sickness would be cured when shamans who practised healing took psychedelic drugs. For example the Mexican Mazatec Indian women use mushrooms to help them into an altered consciousness and then they are supposedly able to 'see' the illness which is afflicting the patient, and the possible cure.

Shamans have been active in Korea, before Buddhism, in Peru as healers, in Siberia, in Indonesia, Tibet and Japan, as well as in Colombia, where shamanism is still widely practised, and in Nepal and Mexico. The underlying thread which links all these diverse cultures over many thousands of years is that of the forces of nature and a belief in the spirit world as an ally in seeing the future. The calling of a shaman is to awaken the spirit within herself/himself and to show others the potential of the connecting worlds and the spiritual futures.

■ *What you can do*

Look for signs of modern shamanism in stories, myths and legends. Read *The Shaman and the Magician* by Nevill Drury (Routledge & Kegan Paul, 1982).

Spiritualism

Spiritualism is a religion. Spiritualists are people who talk to those who have died through the psychic channelling of mediums. Spiritualism was a craze in the USA in the middle 1880s and there was estimated to be over 15,000 mediums operating at any one time talking to and producing messages, drawings and paintings. Daniel Douglas Home was the most famous spiritualist of that era and he regularly was able to produce levitations, rappings, and discussions with those who have deceased.

Modern spiritualism is encompassed in the search for knowledge about ourselves and the planet and a number of mediums have produced work of great meaning and philosophical importance channelled from the spirit world.

See also MEDIUMS, CHANNELLING, PSYCHIC, HYPNOSIS.

Read *Soul to Soul* magazine and *Spirit Speaks*, regular magazines of channelled information and teachings. See addresses at the end.

Superstitions

The belief that forces, either natural or supernatural control our lives is shown in millions of people's faith in superstitions. These are commonly thought to be 'old wives' tales' or stories and myths passed down from one generation to another. In medieval and later times they took on significance, as witchcraft and other pagan religions were thought to be dangerous and anyone who came into contact with witches and their so-called unknown forces had to protect themselves with unknown energies. We can trace all manner of seemingly silly practices back to this era – like crossing fingers, wearing garlic, throwing salt over your shoulder, only allowing a dark-haired person in your house first at New Year, wearing rosemary at weddings but not ivy, and so forth.

Superstitious people look everywhere for meaning and symbolism in the things that happen to them. In the wave of New Age spiritualism this is now called 'hearing whispers from your higher self'. People claim that their seemingly irrational fears or problems can be explained by past lives and the unfinished karma of events that happened perhaps thousands of years ago.

Nonetheless, superstitious beliefs exist and they hold much weight for many people in all cultures. Some are built on sound natural laws, like weather systems and coming storms; others on luck and bad judgement.

■ *What you can do*

Notice the superstitious beliefs your family hold. What are they built on? Can you find the original meanings of these fears and beliefs?

Notice how these superstitions vary from culture to culture. How are they linked together?

Read *A Dictionary of Superstitions*, edited by Iona Opie and Moira Tatem (Oxford University Press, 1989) for a fascinating historical perspective on much of the British use of superstitious folklore.

See also WITCHES AND WITCHCRAFT, MYTHS AND LEGENDS, FOLK TALES AND FABLES.

Taoism

Taoism is a Chinese philosophy founded by Lao-Tzu about 2,600 years ago. The scripture that he wrote, the *Tao Te Ching* (The Way of Power), has become a classic, and has been printed more times than the Bible. Laughter makes up a large part of the path of Taoism and simplicity of lifestyle and thought are vitally important.

There is no known translation for the word 'Tao', but it is defined as the 'way' or 'path' that we travel in our lives. Like Zen Buddhism, it considers the way we do things to be as important as the final result. Finding Tao within you means you find enlightenment and perfection and also an order in your individual life that harmonises with the universe.

The most famous work in Taoism is the *Book of the Way* by Lao-Tzu. The two current schools of Taoism don't specifically follow the mysticism of his work, but keep the basic energy of the idea. The ultimate goal of Taoism is personally to achieve *wu-wei*, a state of perfection, harmony and simplicity, by doing nothing.

■ *What you can do*

The most enjoyable book on Taoism must be *The Tao of Pooh*, by Benjamin Hoff (1972).

Tarot Cards

The earliest surviving tarot cards were produced in Italy in 1400. Mystery surrounds their origins, and some stories and myths say that they originated in Atlantis or ancient Egypt, but no evidence has been produced to back this up. What is clear is that the cards use symbols and meanings that date back much further than 1400 in Europe. The images found on the cards – the world, death, temperance, judgement, the Devil, etc. – all conjure up the sentiments and understanding of the self that is so popular in divination of any sort.

The symbolic illustrations on each of the 78 tarot cards offer an understanding of the psychological world that is revealed by no other method of divination. Each card's meaning is complex and expressive; only the *I Ching* has a method more difficult to understand. The hundreds of sets of cards available today often make brilliant and artistic use of symbolism. They can be collected for their artistic beauty as well as the deep meaning of their divine messages of and what the future holds.

One common theory of how tarot became so widely used and known is the story of the occultist Etteila, who copied Antoine Court de Gebelin's idea to spread the Book of Thoth, the Egyptian God. Another theory is that they evolved from the use of unbound 'picture' books which told mystical tales and spiritual stories to people who couldn't read.

Tarot cards have also been called 'the compendium of gypsy philosophy and religion' and they have flourished throughout Europe in minor religions for the past 500 years. In 1378 the cards were banned in Germany; in 1397 in Paris, and in 1441 in Venice. In 1423 St Bernadino declared that they were invented by the Devil, and churchmen were especially enraged by the Major Arcana, the 22 picture cards which head up the other sets of four houses numbered one to ten.

The tarot cards painted by the artist Bonifacio Bembo as a wedding present for the Italian noble families of Visconti and Sforza depicted a female Pope as one of the Major Arcana cards. In 1300 the Catholic Church had burned Maria Visconti to death for being elected the very first woman Pope by a group of heretics.

The tarot has been linked to many mystical systems such as the qabalah and classical paganism, and to the Eastern philosophy of hiding secrets and myths within pictures so that they can reveal their true identity only to a believer. The Major Arcana in the tarot represent symbols which correspond to the 22 paths found in the qabalistic Tree of Life discovered by the occultist Eliphas Levi in the nineteenth century.

When the Church failed to eradicate tarot cards, commonly used tactics were employed: the cards were converted whenever possible to Christian principles. Thus the Major Arcana was pronounced to be the stations of the cross from the journey which Jesus took before he was crucified. This didn't work for long though, as the cards had deep significant meanings that were fundamentally opposed to Christian ideas. They were based on the elements of the earth, on the qualities of pleasures, virtues, riches and cleanliness or virginities and on an understanding of Eastern definitions of the stages of life.

To read tarot effectively you need 50 per cent intuition and 50 per cent understanding of the system. They are long and complex to learn but if you are interested your friends may not mind if you read tarot books while you try!

■ *What you can do*

When you have chosen your own tarot pack keep it safe and protected. Wrap your cards in a silk scarf. Don't use anyone else's as the energy from other people's cards will mingle in with your own and you want them to be as clean and clear of psychic debris as possible so that you can pick up vibrations and intuitive understanding from them. Hold them often, thinking, meditating and concentrating on them. Take one card for a day and get to know it, read everything that is written about that particular card, look carefully at the depiction, feel and sense what you can from the card, writing anything of interest down in your journal. You can then 'tune in' to the cards and your readings will be more successful.

When you do a reading, let the enquirer shuffle the cards for a short while and ask a question that needs to be answered. Then they cut the pack twice and you deal out the show, or spread, in order to read it. Never go straight into the reading doing each card one by one; always get a sense of the whole picture before you speak, judging the possible outcomes of your reading.

Never deliberately or intentionally hurt anyone by doing a reading. You should never insist that the cards hold the answers, and that these must be acted upon. They only hold one possible answer and an enquirer can make up her own mind about her possible future. Get yourself more than one good book on the tarot. They vary so much that you should get an overall feeling from as many sources as possible before you make pronouncements on what this or that card means. Check within yourself if the stated meaning of the card 'feels' right – this probably means more than the words on the paper!

Read *The Women's Spirituality Book*, by Diane Stein (Llewellyn, 1987) for an eco-feminist view; and *The World Atlas of Divination*, by John Matthews (Eddison Sadd, 1992).

Telepathy

Telepathic experiences take place without obvious communication such as words or writing; instead communication comes directly from the mind. It is the direct transmission of thought from one person to another. The word 'telepathy' has been used to describe various psychic experiences for a long time and is one of the most vigorously experimented with of all the psychic phenomena.

In Colin Wilson's *Beyond the Occult* the author describes dozens of well documented and witnessed examples of telepathy and its effects, including that of the writer J. B. Priestley who was attending a boring literary dinner and decided to pick the most sombre-looking woman in the room and 'make' her wink at him. He did this with some success, by merely concentrating on the woman and suggesting telepathically to her that she should look at him and make the suggestive movement.

The largest ever known experiment in telepathy was in 1971 when the rock group Grateful Dead played concerts in New York while a specific image was shown to the audience of several thousands. The audience were asked to concentrate on this picture and see if they could transmit it to Malcolm Bessant, an English psychic who was asleep some 50 miles away. Four out of six of the images were specifically and correctly explained by the psychic, who obtained the information via his dreams.

Most telepathic experiences use more than just telepathy, often combining it with the psychic use of ESP (extrasensory perception) to achieve the most dramatic results. As ESP includes clairvoyance, the ability to 'see', as well as clairaudience, the ability to 'hear', and other similar forms of ESP the use of telepathy alone is more infrequent.

Most telepathic experiments are carried out using Zener cards, which were designed by the American scientist J. B. Rhine in the 1920s. The cards consist of five symbols: a cross, circle, box, wavy lines, and a five-pointed star. The cards are shuffled and the person doing the experiment picks one card and concentrates on it while the psychic tries to read the information to make a positive identification.

■ *What you can do*

Experiment with telepathy. Concentrate on a subject, picture, number or colour and try to 'transmit' that information from your own mind to the mind of your friend. Notice if the experiment works better with someone whom you are in close contact with, or with someone you don't know so well. Does meditation and concentration affect your results?

Devise experiments with playing cards and see if you can 'tell' which card your friend is holding and thinking of. Results will increase dramatically if you are in a semi-meditative state. Try it both ways and see if there is a difference. Like all psychic phenomena the art of telepathy will only increase with practice and concentration.

See also CLAIRVOYANCE, MEDITATION.

Third Eye

The place from where our psychic projection stems is known as the third eye. If you are clairvoyant for instance you might start to see pictures from your third eye, which sits at the centre of your brow or forehead. This is of course not the only place from which you can have spiritual or psychic experiences but it is the centre of the pineal gland and the place where the chakra is situated which opens access to psychic and similar experiences.

Any work on psychic opening or awakening will stimulate

the third eye and care should be taken that, along with the rest of the chakras and the aura, it is closed down after any such work, including meditation.

■ *What you can do*

Read *The Opening of the Third Eye*, by Douglas Baker (Aquarian, 1977).

See CHAKRAS, AURA, PSYCHIC and PROTECTION.

Unidentified Flying Objects (UFOs)

UFOs have caused a stir in the media since the 1940s, when hundreds of cases of strange lights were spotted by civilians and airforce personnel on both sides during the war. At least one of these strange airships has since been exposed by the tireless and diligent UFO researcher, John Keel, as a Japanese balloon but the search for a reasonable explanation of thousands of other strange sightings still continues.

In Jenny Randle's excellent book *UFOs and How to See Them* some of the most convincing explanations are at hand. Randle's painstaking work has exposed and dissected many of the photographs claimed to be of UFOs over the years. She claims that most UFOs are actually IFOs (Identified Flying Objects) and the proof is clear. Airships, balloons and aeroplanes lit up in the twilight or photographed through windows can often cause strange reflections and look like something from outer space, and even street lights and reflections from cars and floodlights play a role. Strange, often small cloud formations can also be mistaken for UFOs and optical illusions are commonplace when people are unclear about exactly what they saw.

However, UFO-type objects are found throughout history and certainly before the invention and use of cameras and film. In Egypt, about 1500 BC there were reports of 'fire circles' in the sky, as well as in South America, India, the Middle East and throughout Europe.

Since the 1940s many people, especially in the United

States, have claimed meetings with the aliens in UFO craft. At first stories described them as arriving from Mars and Venus but as science crept ever nearer to exploration of these planets the emphasis switched to either the astral planes (see ASTRAL PLANE) of these planets or to other solar systems thousands of light-years away.

While sceptics argue about whether the evidence is faked or tampered with, it's probably best to keep an open mind. If there are 200 billion stars out there with planets circling them then there is a fairly good chance that at least one or two might have some forms of life on them. It would be arrogant in the extreme to think life exists only on our planet. It is also clear from meetings with angels and spirits that there is some form of life, or at least conscious thought, out there which isn't like our own.

In the USA the work of the novelist Whitley Strieber has increased the tension between the sceptics and the believers even further. His novel *Communion* suggests that visitors from outer space have been abducting members of the public in order to carry out experiments, and even brainwashing them. There are now many people who regularly attend therapy sessions where they talk about their experiences. These claims have been argued to be manipulative and divisive, however, and no proof has ever been brought forward to back them up, although questions still need to be answered.

The United States government and other governments around the world do take the question of UFOs seriously enough to have set up their own departments and investigation units on the subject, which often operate secretly within the CIA, Ministry of Defence or some other secret service. It could be either that they know something we don't or that they genuinely want to find out but for obvious reasons don't want everyone to know!

■ *What you can do*

Read the excellent journal *Fortean Times* which documents strange phenomena and UFO sightings from an interested but sceptical standpoint (see MAGAZINES). Read Jenny Randle's *UFOs and How to See Them* (Anaya, 1993).

Learn to look in the sky. If you want to be a UFO-spotter

start to concentrate on the sky as much as you can; you'd be surprised at how often we look only straight ahead or down. Carry a camera with you as often as you can and practise taking night and long-distance pictures.

The visibility of a UFO might not be clear, and it may be moving fast, so as well as taking pictures it's a good idea to draw what you saw or immediately write down a detailed account. Things to note are the exact time, location, angle, particular cloud formations/weather patterns at the time, and any visible colours or shapes.

If you are convinced about what you saw you could contact your local police station so that a formal sighting can be recorded, but you might get a better reception by joining or contacting one of the many UFO groups in the UK or sending your pictures to the *Fortean Times*.

Jenny Randle will answer letters and give advice if you send a SAE to her at 37 Heathbank Road, Cheadle Heath, Stockport, Cheshire SK3 0UP.

Unconditional Love

Why is a topic like unconditional love in a book like this? For me it is quite simple: unconditional love represents the most powerful form of magic there is. Everything else can be transformed, changed, shaped and created with this amazing energy.

It's not the same sort of love that you feel for the boy down the road who wants to take you out, or the love you feel for your family; unconditional love is much deeper than that. It is, essentially, loving something, somebody without judging them (judging is the bit of you that thinks she's all right but I don't like her clothes/accent/hairstyle/manners, etc.) and without wanting anything in return.

All the major religions talk about love overcoming the world's problems in one way or another, and it's true if you practise it. Try this experiment in a crowded shopping centre or restaurant. Try to stay very still, and decide to connect yourself, lovingly, to each person in your view. Then imagine that the love you have created goes past everyone you can see and to all the shoppers or people eating at restaurants that you can't see. Imagine that everyone you can sense is connected to you, and that you love them without conditions attached. Notice yourself looking critically at someone undesirable in your mind and continue to spread the loving feeling towards that person, who is, after all, connected to you. This can be practised everywhere with great effect.

When you are next at a party or get-together and you feel uncomfortable with people, practise feeling unconditional love towards them and see what changes – you or them? Don't open yourself to abuse with this practice; loving people doesn't mean that they can walk all over you. It means opening your heart and accepting them and loving them for what they are.

■ *What you can do*

Practise this magic everywhere you can: the energy of unconditional love spreads fast. Imagine smiling at the bus conductor and watch as they suddenly feel lighter and smile at other passengers. Smile at checkout assistants and watch their misery evaporate. This sort of magic is more powerful than anything and even small groups of people doing it can make a huge difference.

Practise random acts of kindness and selfless acts of beauty. A woman in the United States has started a movement dedicated to practising unconditional love in secret. She began by paying the toll fee on the motorway for the five cars behind her, and the idea spread fast. People have been carrying out random acts of kindness, including planting flowers and bulbs in public places, putting money into car meters in the street if the cars are just about to get a parking ticket, and generally being beautiful in secret. See if you can carry out such acts yourself.

Read *Living Magically*, by Gill Edwards (Piatkus, 1991), and *Random Acts of Kindness* (Conari Press, 1993).

See JESUS, MAGIC, VISUALISATION.

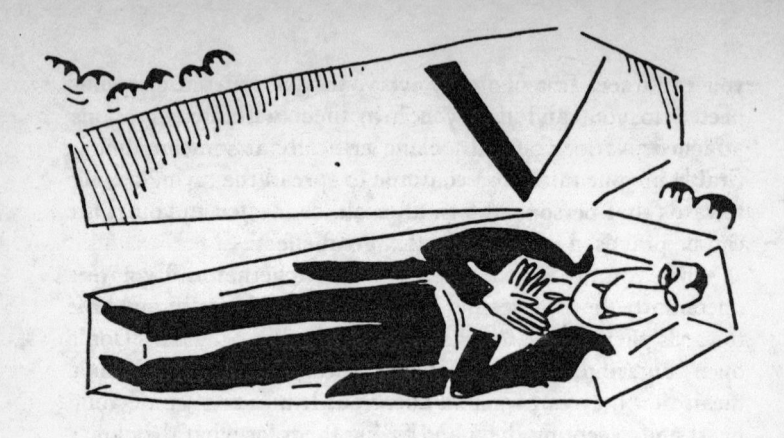

Vampires

Vampires... the very name can produce shivers in the spine. Anyone who has seen Count Dracula movies will know that vampires are reportedly responsible for sucking blood from the necks of their victims, producing anaemic and depleted people who in turn have to revive themselves by attacking others in the same way.

While Bram Stoker's *Dracula* (1897) is of course a good story, there is an element of truth in vampirism from a psychic perspective. There have indeed been cases of psychic vampirism with or without the blood-sucking! Everyone knows of someone who drains them, someone who makes them feel ill and sleepy, even exhausted. These people can, consciously or, as with most cases, unconsciously, suck vital energy from the aura of the people around them, depleting them slowly and deliberately. Dion Fortune rightly says this is more like parasitism than vampirism, and in *Psychic Self-Defence* she claims that such action is extremely widespread and the basis of many common psychological problems.

She goes on to describe one of the only cases of true vampirism from a psychic perspective that have been reported. It involved dead and dying soldiers who were on the front line during the First World War. Some of these soldiers, who practised occult arts, knew how to project their etheric body into the astral plane and so were not willing to die but hung around people as ghosts, feeding off them by sucking blood and energy from any victim they came across. Even though one or two were technically dead, they were able to spread their vampire activities to others by 'infecting' them.

The word 'vampire' is Slavic and probably originated in India, but the Greek word, according to Barbara Walker the feminist writer, is *sarcomenos*, meaning 'flesh made by the moon'. The connection with the moon is long-standing and it is thought that vampires needed to use the moon to provide them with the energy that we as humans associate with the sun. There were even myths and superstitions in the Middle Ages that said if a woman were to sleep naked at full moon she would become pregnant and give birth to a vampire child!

While vampires have been linked to demonology and black magic there is no real evidence to back this up other than they were (and possibly still are today) people who preferred to use their bodies to keep them earthbound and to try and defy death using any occult practices they could. The vampire seems like a sad and frightened person who cannot pass through physical death to the other worlds and needs to feed off others to keep his or her body half dead and half alive.

■ *What you can do*

In the extremely unlikely event that you come into contact with a vampire try psychic protection (see PROTECTION), try a stake through the heart, try garlic, try a therapist, try moving house!

You can easily catch up with the ideas on what vampires are supposed to do to you if you want to be frightened by watching a good Dracula movie.

If you think you are around people who act like psychic parasites then there are things you can do:

- Protect yourself whenever you are near them by closing your aura (see AURA, PROTECTION).
- After an encounter in which you feel tired or drained give yourself a psychic shower to cleanse their energy from your body and then imagine a new, stronger aura enveloping you and protecting you.
- Ask your guides to help in this protection.
- Ask yourself why you hang around with people like this.

Read *Vampires, Burial and Death*, by Paul Barber (Yale University Press, 1988); *Psychic Self-Defence and Well-Being*, by Melita

Denning and Osborne Phillips (Llewellyn, 1993) and Dion Fortune's *Psychic Self-Defence*.

Contact the Vampyre Society, which is concerned with the cultural aspects of vampirism.

See ETHERIC BODY, ASTRAL PLANE.

Visualisation

Visualisation means using your mind to create pictures. Just sit as you read this book and imagine you are holding a flower. What colour is it? How long is the stem? How many leaves has it? Notice the petals: are they all one colour or many shades?

If you managed to see anything at all then you can use visualisation techniques to help you. It can take practice but almost everyone can perform some level of positive visualisation whenever they relax and concentrate enough.

Athletes use visualisation to enhance their performances, often 'seeing' themselves winning a race, jumping over the bar or finishing a routine with ease. Of course they all have to train and practise as well to make sure that their physical bodies are in top shape, but their mental images of themselves are what can give them the edge over another competitor. Many sports managers and trainers know that the chances of success for their students can be changed almost instantaneously by thought processes working positively in their favour.

Students of Hung Kuen, the ancient martial art of China developed some 2,000 years ago, use visualisation techniques to enhance their precision. They must undergo rigorous training, including the study and observation of animals in their natural habitats so that the movement and style of the animal will inspire natural actions in the student.

Other forms of visualisation include imagining yourself surrounded by colours that you need to protect or enhance you (see also PSYCHIC, PROTECTION); spreading good thoughts and deeds using images of flowers or rainbows flowing from your body; preparing yourself for an operation in hospital by imagining waking up feeling well and better; absorbing white light into your body each time you take a breath; creating a small army of 'fixers' to heal or stitch a wound; and swallowing a star just before you begin to undertake any activity that requires large amounts of energy.

All of these visualisations and techniques can help make your life positive. You don't have to believe in any religion or special form of magic to make it work; just by using the power of your mind you can reverse bad luck and create opportunities for good. The more specific you are the better the results too!

■ *What you can do*

Develop your imagination whenever you can; use your mind to imagine yourself as an angel, as Robin Hood, an eagle, a computer or a book. Such imagination is the underlying basis for entry to the mythical world, where you can have enormous fun, no matter how old or young you are. This will also increase your mental powers and allow you to use more difficult visualisation techniques to your advantage.

Visualise yourself carrying out an activity that you like – swimming, or playing football or hockey, for instance – then create the situation in your mind that allows you to feel the wind in your hair, smell the sweat on your body, taste the orange or drink you got at half-time, touch the ball, or the grass. Recreating such schemes in your mind will mean that you use and teach yourself important skills, stretching visualisation beyond what you see to cover all your senses.

Choose a goal that you want to achieve; perhaps passing an exam or acquiring a new bicycle. Make sure that your goal is clear, possible (not a million pounds by Friday!), available, means something to you and stretches your capability. Be futuristic – determine *when* you will achieve the effect. Then ensure that you have carried out all the obvious (and often boring!) types of research that will lead you to your goal, like revision for instance, detailing the times and actions that you will have to achieve in order to reach your goal. For instance, say your goal is to meet a new boyfriend. You won't get one easily by staying indoors each evening; your plan could include going out more often with different groups of people, to unusual places. All your plans, like the final goal itself, must be realistic and achievable.

Now you can begin to use extra visualisation techniques to help you reach your goal. Get yourself into a relaxed state (see MEDITATION for ideas). When you are relaxed, let your mind take you to the future, to the place or person that you wish to be. Your subconscious mind will help you by throwing up pictures that you can work on. The most important thing is to imagine yourself in the position you want to be in. Don't look on at someone else that you admire for doing it; imagine *you* are doing it – feel it, smell it, touch it. Once you have in mind the feeling of success you can revisualise it whenever possible.

If you find negative feelings coming up for you, like I'm not good enough, I'm not pretty/thin/tall/black/intelligent, etc. then look at your self-esteem and use affirmations to rebalance your life, making it a positive experience for you, not for others around you.

Here's good visualisation to get you up in the morning. When you are lying down preparing to sleep the night before, count backwards from ten down to nought very slowly. Then visualise a large clock with hands at the time you wish to wake up in the morning, say 7 a.m., and repeat in your mind, 'At 7 a.m. I will wake up', three times. Then go to sleep and see the results very quickly!

Read Ronald Shone's *Creative Visualization* (Thorsons, 1984) and *Living Magically*, and *Stepping into the Magic*, by Gill Edwards (Piatkus 1991 and 1993).

Notice the words you use every day – do they empower your desires and your creative visualisations? It's no good wanting to swim in the next Olympics if you tell everyone you meet that you aren't very good at it! Try to be positive without showing off, and make your words match the work that your mind is creating.

Use visualisations in meditation to enhance your experience and your spirtuality. Guided visualisation tapes can be purchased by mail order. These offer you help with studying, losing weight, building self-esteem and overcoming many other emotional and negative blocks.

You can also use guided meditation to meet your personal spirit guides and communicate with them. See MEDITATION, GUARDIAN ANGELS OR GUIDES.

Voodoo

Few religions have been so misunderstood and victimised as voodoo. The word itself evokes fear and revulsion in many people – stories of Africans who are possessed, witch doctors, black magic, potions and dangerous charms abound, but these are nearly always told by negative and narrow-minded bigots who fail to understand a central and important religious group in Africa which dates back many centuries.

The word 'voodoo' itself comes from the Fon people in Africa, and means creative genius and protective spirit, but also foresight.

In Haiti, the home of voodoo religions in the West Indies, Africans were brought as slaves to the Americas and the Negro population created its own form of religious symbolism that has largely been the subject of so much derision from Christians and other religious groups.

The religion itself is built on simple principles: priestesses and priests are trained to 'channel' information of use to others from the dead ancestors of the group. The consciousness of the ancestors is called Egus and the consciousness of the spirit of nature and natural phenomena like the wind, ocean and fire is called Orishas. Many of the spirits come into the body of the priests not when they are sitting at a darkened table like mediums in Europe, but through the power of dance and the drum. Anyone who has felt the energy of a drumbeat through their body must understand the frenzy and rhythm of the dance. This frenzy will develop into a trance, and the ancestral spirits will enter the priestess's body. During these possessions healing of both mind and body can take place. Voodoo is not used for black magic. The respected historian W. B. Seabrook wrote in *The Magic Island* (1929) that any bloodshed in voodoo ceremonies is almost certainly to be an offering of an animal to the ancestors and gods no different to the offerings made in the Bible and by the druids all over Europe.

Voodoo is used mainly to counter evil forces, to help healing, to protect people on journeys and to increase awareness within. Most of the negative stories regarding such an intense religion came from racist and fearful Christians who declared any god not their own to be heathen, and those who took part in voodoo ceremonies to be practising black magic.

■ *What you can do*

Look out for instances where voodoo is used to undermine Africans and counteract it with your own knowledge whenever you can. Read *Jambalya: The Natural Woman's Book of Personal Charms and Practical Rituals* (Llewellyn, 1982); this is written by Luisah Teish, voodoo high priestess in the USA.

Werewolves

Werewolves, like vampires, owe their notoriety more to modern films and horror stories than to actual cases. The origins of the werewolf are in early societies and cults who worshipped their gods in wolf form. The wolf spirit is said to have many great powers, both masculine and feminine, and werewolves appear in Greek myths and other stories.

It is said that the werewolf is a woman or man who can transform herself or himself into the body of a wolf to devour the flesh of enemies. Lycanthropy is the name given to such practices but it is more likely that occult practitioners and shamans knew how to transform themselves by using herbs, hallucinogenic drugs and occult methods to become attuned with their spirit animal or their totem.

Barbara Walker has studied and reported only a few cases of lycanthropy in Europe, over the centuries. One man, Peter Stubb of Cologne, was tortured until he confessed to having been in league with the devil and transforming himself into a werewolf. He was brutally tortured by having the flesh pulled off his bones with red-hot pincers. His legs and arms were broken with a wooden axe, and finally he was beheaded and burned. This was of course during the Inquisition of the sixteenth century.

■ *What you can do*

Notice your fears and prejudices about mythology and werewolves and your feelings about wolves and animals.

Read Barry Holstun Lopez's touching work *Of Wolves and Men* (Charles Scribner's Sons, 1978), which gives a modern and historical perspective on our relationship to wolves.

Witches and Witchcraft

Witches, women with psychic powers, women healers, midwives, clairvoyants, herbalists, counsellors and wise women – all these women have been accused of the religion of witchcraft in the last 300 years. Patriarchy (male power systems) has shown a bias against women and men who practised earth-based religions like paganism and wicca, or witchcraft. Even today many people have failed to see that witches are not in league with the Devil any more than the priests of our modern religions are. 'Witch' has even become used as a derogatory word for 'woman' by people who don't want to swear in public!

In the witch-burning times from the fourteenth to the eighteenth century both Catholics and Protestants were responsible for the hysteria and mass killing of women and men for the 'crime' of being a witch. Witch-hunting was a profitable business, and once a woman was accused it was difficult to find anyone who would speak up for her, lest they be accused as well. It is estimated that between 100,000 and 5 million people were tortured, burned at the stake, hung, drawn and quartered for this crime. The historian George Lincoln Barr found records of a minimum of 100,000 killings in Germany alone. Most of those who died were women. Misogyny, the hatred of women, was at its height. In the last hundred years many people have done the same thing to Jews during the Second World War: millions went to concentration camps and gas chambers in Europe.

There are stories of witches murdered for confessing to crimes they could never have committed, such was the pain of torture. Women were killed for keeping bees and producing honey, which was said to be the work of the Devil. Women who practised herbalism and healing suddenly found themselves in competition with men who practised a new form of medicine and wanted money for it – so it was convenient that they be accused of witchcraft and executed. In one town in

Germany such was the hysteria that not one single woman survived. Women lost their property, their belongings, their families and their lives. Even children who were born to women witches could be burned, and mothers were accused of witchcraft if anything happened to their offspring. In June 1722 the last recorded witch-burning took place in Scotland when Janet Horne was burned for having lamed her daughter by means of the craft, according to Doreen Valiente, one of today's witches who is willing to be identified.

Witchcraft is one of the fastest-growing religions in Britain today and paganism, and druidism have similarities in their methods and motives. Their followers are not devil-worshippers but nature-worshippers, tuning in to the cycles of the sun and moon, calling on gods and goddesses to work their magic with them.

One of the laws of witchcraft is that whatever you do comes back to you three times, and this law operates as an important reminder of the connectedness and karma of any magical work. There are witches and magicians that call upon the Devil, but they are few and hard to find, and practise their ugly magic for power without thought to their futures.

■ *What you can do*

Watch yourself and your inbuilt prejudices. Do you use the term witch as a form of abuse? Notice the language and bigotry of others. Would you call someone you didn't like a Jew or Hindu? Why a witch?

If you want to become a witch start with reading good earth magic books, not ones that laugh at the idea of wiccan religion. Try *A Witch Alone; Thirteen Moons to Master Natural Magic*, by Marian Green (Aquarian, 1991); *The Crone's Book of Words*, by Valerie Worth (Llewellyn, 1988); *An ABC of Witchcraft Past and Present*, by Doreen Valiente (Robert Hale, 1973); Colin Wilson's *Beyond the Occult* (Corgi, 1988); *Good Magic*, by Marina Medici (Prentice-Hall, 1988); *The Women's Spirituality Book*, by Diane Stein (Llewellyn, 1987); *The Complete Art of Witchcraft*, by Sybil Leek (Signet New Age, 1971); *The Spiral Dance*, by Starhawk (Harper & Row, 1979); and *The Women's Press Book of New Myth and Magic*, edited by Helen Windrath (Women's Press, 1993).

Find ways to heal society from the witch-burning times; start talking about it and discussing it whenever you can. Support women's initiatives to commemorate those who have died, and think of your own.

See also HEALING, PAGANISM, DRUIDS, PSYCHIC, HERBS.

Yoga

The practice of yoga is over 4,000 years old and the word is thought to be derived from the ancient Sanskrit which means 'union'. The union is the merging, through spiritual practice, of the individual soul with the universal soul, through a process of self-realisation.

Yoga is much more than the stretching and bending exercises that you may have seen; full yoga practices can be complex and require dedication. Meditation, knowledge and use of energy systems, including the chakras and Hinduism, form only the basis. Yoga is a deeply revered spiritual practice which enables the body, mind and spirit to be bound together through love and spiritual wisdom.

There are at least ten versions of yoga in current use around the world. Hatha Yoga is the most widely practised in Europe and North America and, as such, concentrates on the path towards health. Patanjali, widely known as the sage of yoga, says there are eight parts of hatha yoga that must be observed: abstinence (*yamas*); observance (*niyamas*); posture (*asanas*), breath control (*pranayama*), sense withdrawal (*pratyahara*), concentration (*dhrana*), contemplation (*dhyana*) and self-realisation (*samadhi*). With these in mind the six purification processes or shat karma are added.

In order to practise yoga as a spiritual path students are expected to undertake certain agreements about personal conduct including : non-violence, vegetarianism, truthfulness, honesty, chastity, and not receiving gifts. All sexual energy is transformed into spiritual energy. Purity is also an important part of the practising yogi, and eating pure (sattwic) food, attention to cleanliness and meditation to cleanse the mind are vital.

Yoga postures, called *asanas*, are physical exercises which improve both the mind and body. They actively promote the health and efficiency of internal organs, the limbs and suppleness of the body, they sharpen the nerves and ensure low blood pressure and a clear heart and mind.

■ *What you can do*

Yoga is a beautiful spiritual practice that has offered many individuals hope, health and physical awareness. Yoga classes are held in many community centres and education centres around the country. While you won't often be pressed to sign up to all the dedicated observances of the yogi, you might like to bear them in mind when you are beginning to practise this ancient art.

Read the *Yoga Journal*, available from good bookshops and wholefood shops.

Join training centres like those listed in ADDRESSES TO CONTACT.

See also MEDITATION, BREATH.

Zen

Buddhist monks in Japan formulated their own version of the teachings of Shakyamuni Buddha, called Zen. It is a practice in which meditation plays an important role, but so does contemplative action. Every action taken by a Zen master is a move towards enlightenment; it is not the end result that is important but the process.

Zen was introduced to Japan by monks returning from China, but it is thought to originate from India.

Zen masters are adept at many skills, including martial arts and painting. Zen paintings are known for their simplicity and fluid beauty; they are those Japanese paintings prepared with black ink that cannot be painted over. Every previous line is a symbol of a life that is visible, every action being important for the path. A Zen artist is revered for he or she creates beauty, and that beauty, because it is perfect, assists people to see the Godforce in all things.

One of the many important implications of living a Zen lifestyle is to be simple and conscious of every action.

■ *What you can do*

Read *Zen*, by Anne Bancroft (1989); *Zen and the Art of Motorcycle Maintenance*, by Robert Pirsig (1979); *Zen Comics*, by Salajan (1993) and *Zen Philosophy*, by Thich Thien An (1989).

Practise the art of being conscious in every wakeful action.
See BUDDHISM, BREATH, MEDITATION.

Short Booklist

Here is a list of some of the best books available to whet your appetite further, especially if you can't think where to start!

Barbara Ann Brennan, *Hands of Light: A Guide to Healing through the Human Energy Field* (Bantam New Age, 1988)

Sophy Burnham, *A Book of Angels* (Ballantine Books, 1990)

Egar Cayce, *Mysteries of the Mind* (Aquarian, 1990)

Thomas Cleary, *I Ching: The Book of Changes* (Shambhala, 1992)

Melita Denning and Osborne Phillips, *Psychic Self-Defence and Well-Being* (Llewellyn, 1980)

Gill Edwards, *Living Magically* (Piatkus, 1991)

Shirley MacLaine, *Out on a Limb* (Bantam Books, 1983)

R. Michael Miller and Josephine Harper, *The Psychic Energy Workbook: An Illustrated Course in Practical Psychic Skills* (Aquarian, 1987)

Melvin Morse, *Closer to the Light: Learning From the Near Death Experiences of Children* (Souvenir, 1991)

Betty Shine *Mind Waves* (Corgi, 1994)

Starhawk, *The Spiral Dance* (Harper & Row, 1979)

Diane Stein, *The Women's Spirituality Book* (Llewellyn, 1987)

Dora van Gelder, *The Real World of Fairies* (Theosophical Publishing House, 1977)

Colin Wilson, *Beyond the Occult* (Corgi, 1988)

Bookshops

Listed below are the bookshops in Britain which are most likely to stock the books recommended here.

Arcania Books
17 Union Passage, Bath BA1 1RE
0225 461687

Arcturus
47 Fore Street, Totnes, Devon TQ9 5NJ
0803 864363

Body & Soul
52 Hamilton Place, Edinburgh EH3 5AX
031 226 3066

Changes Bookshop
242 Belsize Road, London NW6 4BT
071 328 5161

Compendium
234 Camden High Street, London NW1 8QS
071 485 8944/267 1525

Gothic Image
7 High Street, Glastonbury, Somerset BA6 9DP
0458 831453
fax: 0458 831666

The Inner Bookshop
34 Cowley Road, Oxford, OX4 1HZ
0865 245301

The Phoenix Centre
The Park, Findhorn, Forres, Morayshire IV36 0TZ
0309 690110
fax: 0309 690933

Watkins Books Ltd
19 and 21 Cecil Court, London, WC2N 4EZ
071 836 2182
fax: 071 836 6700

Magazines

Caduceus
38 Russell Terrace, Leamington Spa,
Warwickshire CV31 1HE
0926 451 897
(Health and healing)

Cerealogist
Specialist Knowledge Services,
Saint Aldhelm, 20 Paul Street,
Frome, Somerset BA11 1DX
0373 451777
(Crop circle studies)

Fortean Times
Box 2409, London, NW5 4NP
071 485 5002
(Strange phenomena)

Human Potential
5 Layton Road, London, N1 0PX
071 354 5792
(Growth and transformation)

1-to-1
92 Prince of Wales Drive, London NW5 3NE
071 267 7094
(Politics/social awareness)

Kindred Spirit
Foxhole, Dartington, Devon TQ9 6EB
0803 866 686
(Health and well-being)

One Earth
The Findhorn Foundation
The Park, Forres, Morayshire IV36 0TZ
0309 691641
(New Age issues)

Prediction

Link House Magazines Ltd
Dingwall Ave, Croydon, Surrey CR9 2TA
081 646 6672
(Fortune-telling)

Psychic News
2 Tavistock Chambers, Bloomsbury Way,
London WC1A 2SE
071 405 3340
(Listings for Spiritualist churches and mediums)

Rainbow Ark
PO Box 486, London, SW1P 1AZ
(New Age listings)

Resurgence
Ford House, Hartland, Bideford, Devon EX39 6EE
0237 441 293
(Green/ecological issues)

The Skeptic
PO Box 475, Manchester M60 2TH
(Scepticism)

Soul to Soul
PO Box 3724, London N16 6HY
(Channelling)

Spirit Speaks
PO Box 84304, Los Angeles, CA 90073–0304
(Spiritual growth)

Addresses to contact

The organisations listed are often small and underfunded. If you are writing to them please enclose a large, stamped addressed envelope if you want to get a reply.

For legal reasons, you may not be allowed to join some of the organisations if you are under 18 years old. Please be aware of the legal implications if you want to join these groups.

Alternatives
St James Church, Piccadilly, London W1V 0LF
071 287 6711

Regular Monday-evening lectures at this very alternative church plus a range of workshops covering laughter, meditation, economics and political spirituality.

ARE Press
67th Street & Atlantic Avenue, PO Box 595,
Virginia Beach, USA
VA 23451–0595

The Astrological Association
396 Caledonian Road, London N1 1DN
071 700 0639

International organisation which acts as the main co-ordinating body of astrology in the UK.

Astrological Association Book Service
101 Herdborough Road, Scarborough,
North Yorkshire YO11 3HP
0723 581765

Bear Tribe Medicine Society
11 Kingscroft Drive, London NW2 3QE
081 450 5459

Disseminates the teaching of Chippewa Medicine Man Sun Bear. Activities include vision quests, pipe ceremonies and workshops.

The British Astrological and Psychic Society
124 Trefoil Crescent, Broadfield, Crawley,
West Sussex RH11 9EZ
0293 54236

Brings together people working or interested in astrology, palmistry, numerology and psychic disciplines.

Brotherhood of Life
110 Dartmouth, SE, Albuquerque, New Mexico,
USA 87106

The Buddhist Society
58 Eccleston Square, London SW1V 1PH
071 834 5858

Celtic Research and Folklaw Society
Spion Kop, Levenlash, Isle of Arran KA27 BNL

College of Psychic Studies
16 Queensberry Place, London, SW7 2EB
071 589 3292

Workshops and lectures on spiritualism, psychic awareness, etc. Costs of workshops vary but are very reasonable.

The Confederation of Healing Organisations
Suite J, The Red & White House, 113 High Street,
Berkhamsted, Hertfordshire HP4 2DJ
0442 870660
Represents leading healing organisations in Britain.

The Council of British Druid Orders
BM Oak Grove
London WC1N 3XX

The Dream Research Centre
8 Willow Road, London NW3
071 794 8717

Runs an ongoing series of workshops in which imaging and the use of symbols play a prominent role. One-to-one sessions are available.

Eagle's Wing Centre for Contemporary Shamanism
58 Westbere Road, London NW2 3RU
071 435 8174

Offers one-year 'Elements of Shamanism' course; also weekend and one-day workshops and talks.

Earth First!
Oxford EF!, Box E, 111 Magdalen Road,
Oxford, OX4 1RQ
0865 201706

Eco-evangelists.

Findhorn Foundation
The Park, Forres, Morayshire IV36 0TZ
0309 691074

Spiritual community with one-week initial personal growth course called the Experience Week and specially organised and cheaper youth programmes.

International Association of Near Death Studies
9 Julier House, Pera Road, Bath BA1 5PA

International Federation of Aromatherapists
c/o Royal Masonic Hospital, Ravenscourt Park,
London W6 0TN

National Federation of Spiritual Healers
Old Manor Farm Studio, Church Street,
Sunbury on Thames, Middlesex TW16 6RG
09327 83164

Can put you in touch with a local healer.

The National Institute of Medical Herbalists
9 Palace Gate, Exeter, Devon EX1 1JA

The Order of Bards, Ovats and Druids
260 Kew Road, Richmond, Surrey TW9 3EG

PaganLink
Box Q, 34 Cowley Road, Oxford OX4 1HZ

Pagan networking organisation putting pagans in touch with each other.

The Pagan Federation
BM Box 7097, London WC1N 3XX

Founded in 1971, this is the largest and oldest pagan body in Europe. Publishes a quarterly journal and has a useful information pack which gives basic facts about paganism. (You must be over 18 to join.)

Pegasus Foundation & School of Channelling
Runnings Park, Croft Bank, West Malvern,
Worcestershire WR14 4BP
0684 573868

Offers series of experiential workshops where you can work with others, under supervision, to exercise your psychic abilities.

Potters (Herbal Supplies)
Leyland Mill Lane, Wigan, Lancashire WN1 2SB

Prana
Tangelynen, Cwm Cou, Newcastle Emlyn,
Dyfed SA38 9PQ
0239 710086

Ethnic chanting group.

Psi Research Centre
14 Selwood Road, Glastonbury, Somerset BA6 8HN

Runnings Park Centre for Healing
Croft Bank, West Malvern, Worcestershire WR14 4BP
0684 565253

Includes a College of Healing offering a three-part diploma course; a school of Channelling offering experiential workshops on your psychic abilities; and the Pegasus Foundation, which focuses on HA channelled teaching.

Saros Foundation
121 Holly Bush Lane, Hampton, Middlesex
TW12 2QY

The School of Herbal Medicine
Bucksteep Manor, Bodle St Green, Hailsham,
East Sussex

Spiritual Association of Great Britain
33 Belgrave Square, London SW1X 8QB
071 235 3351

Church services with mediums, workshops and introductory lessons on spiritualism. Active churches all over the UK.

Sufi Healing Order of Great Britain
29 Grosvenor Place, London Road, Bath,
Avon BA1 6BA
0225 312694

Talking Stick & DRAGON!
3 Sandford Walk, New Cross, London SE14 6NB

Spirituality and ecological magic.

The Temple ov Psychic Youth
PO Box 687, Halfway, Sheffield S19 5UX

Organisation for young people (you must be over 18 to join) interested in psychic music, art chanting and radical ideas.

The Theosophical Society
50 Gloucester Place, London W1H 3HJ

The Vampyre Society
PO Box 68, Keighley, West Yorkshire BD22 6RU

Books to read

An ABC of Witchcraft Past and Present, Doreen Valiente. Robert Hale, 1973

Alchemy: The Medieval Alchemists and their Royal Art, Johannes Fabricius. Aquarian, 1989

The Aquarian Dictionary of Festivals, J. C. Cooper. Aquarian, 1990

Alchemy, Cherry Gilchrist. Element, 1991

Ask Your Angels, Alma Daniel, Timothy Wyllie and Andrew Ramer. Ballantine Books, 1992

The Angel Book: A Handbook for Aspiring Angels, Karen Goldman. Simon & Schuster, 1992

Beyond the Occult, Colin Wilson. Corgi, 1991

A Book of Angels, Sophy Burnham. Ballantine Books, 1990

The Book of Druidry, Ross Nichols. Aquarian, 1990

Diary of a Teenage Psychic, Matthew Manning.

Closer to the Light: Learning from the Near Death Experiences of Children, Melvin Morse. Souvenir, 1991

Commune with the Angels: A Heavenly Handbook, Jane M. Howard. ARE Press, 1992

The Complete Art of Witchcraft, Sybil Leek. Signet New Age, 1971

The Complete Book of Incense, Oils and Brews, Scott Cunningham. Llewellyn, 1991

Creative Visualization, Ronald Shone. Thorsons, 1984

The Crone's Book of Words, Valerie Worth. Llewellyn, 1971

Cunningham's Encyclopedia of Magical Herbs. Llewellyn, 1985

Devas, Fairies and Angels: A Modern Approach, William Bloom. Gothic Image Publications, 1986

Dictionary of Beliefs and Religions. Chambers, 1992

Dictionary of Mysticism and the Esoteric Traditions, Nevill Drury. Prism Unity, 1992

The Diviner's Handbook, Tom Graves. Element, 1988

Dreaming: Remembering, Interpreting, Benefiting, Derek and Julia Parker. Prentice-Hall, 1985

The Druids, Stuart Piggott. Penguin Books, 1974

The Druid Tradition, Philip Carr-Gomm. Element, 1991

Earth Mysteries, Philip Heselton. Element, 1991

Earth Power: Techniques of Natural Magic, Scott Cunningham. Llewellyn, 1983

The Encyclopedia of Gods, Michael Jordan. Kyle Cathie, 1992

Essene Book of Meditations and Blessings, Danaan Parry. Sunstone Publications, 1992

Explaining the Unexplained: Mysteries of the Paranormal, Hans J. Eysenck and Carl Sargent. BCA, 1993

Exploring Reincarnation, Hans TenDam. Arkana, 1990

Fate & Prediction: An Historical Compendium of Astrology, Palmistry and Tarot, Fred Gettings. Ferndale Editions, 1980

The Flood from Heaven: Deciphering the Atlantis Legend, Eberhard Zangger. BCA, 1984

The Forces of Destiny: Reincarnation, Karma and Astrology, Penny Thornton. Weidenfeld & Nicholson, 1990

Fortune Telling by Palmistry: A Practical Guide to the Art of Hand Analysis, Rodney Davies. Aquarian, 1987

Free Rides: How to Get High without Drugs, Douglas Rushkoff and Patrick Wells. Delta Books, 1991

The Ghost Hunters' Almanac: A Guide to over 120 Hauntings, Peter Underwood. Eric Dobby Publishing, 1993

Gildas Communicates, Ruth White and Mary Swainson. C. W. Daniel, 1971

The Goddess Celebrates: An Anthology of Women's Rituals, edited by Diane Stein. Crossing Press, 1991

The Goddesses and Gods of Old Europe: Myths and Cult Images, Marija Gimbutas. University of California Press, 1989

The Goddess of the Stones: The Language of the Megaliths, George Terence Meaden. Souvenir Press, 1991

The Golden Bough: The classic study in magic and religion, J. G. Frazer. Papermac, 1990

Good Magic, Marina Medici. Prentice-Hall, 1988

Greek Myths, Robert Graves. Cassells, 1991

The Guide Book: Where There Is Love. HA on Life and Living. A Channelled Teaching of Our Time, Tony Neate. Pegasus Foundation, 1992

A Handbook of Psychic Protection: Simple and Effective Ways to Surround Yourself with Good Vibrations, Draja Mickaharic. Rider, 1993

Hands of Light: A Guide to Healing through the Human Energy Field, Barbara Ann Brennan. Bantam New Age Books, 1988

Healing Stones, Lorusso and Joe Glick, Brotherhood of Life, 1976

Herbal Medicine, R. F. Weiss. Beaconsfield Press, 1988

A History of Magic, Richard Cavendish. Arkana, 1987

A History of Witchcraft: Sorcerers, Heretics and Pagans, Jeffrey B. Russell. Thames & Hudson, 1977

How to Meditate: A Guide to Self-Discovery, Lawrence LeShan Crucible. Aquarian, 1974

How to Read the Aura: Its Character and Function in Everyday Life, W. E. Butler. Aquarian, 1979

The Hypnotic World of Paul McKenna, Faber & Faber, 1993

The I Ching: Book of Changes, Thomas Cleary. Shambhala, 1992

The Illustrated Encyclopedia of Dreams, Anna Fornari, Emilio Rombaldini and Lynn Picknett. BCA, 1993

The Illustrated Encyclopedia of Myths and Legends, Arthur Cotterell. BCA and Marshall Editions, 1992

The Inner Guide to Meditation, Edwin Steinbrecher. Aquarian, 1982

Inside the Supernatural: An Investigation into the Paranormal, Jean Ritchie. Fontana, 1992

Jambalya: The Natural Woman's Book of Personal Charms and Practical Rituals, Luisah Teish. Llewellyn, 1982

Journey through the Chakras: Exercises for Healing and Internal Balancing, Klahsbernd Vollmar, Gateway Boosk, 1987

The Joy of Aromatherapy, Cathy Hopkins. Angus & Robertson, 1991

Kingdoms of the Gods, Geoffrey Hudson. Theosophical Publishing House, 1970

The Language of the Goddess, Marija Gimbutas. Harper San Francisco, 1989

Life after Life, Raymond Moody. Corgi, 1976

Life and Living: A Channelled Teaching of our Time, H–A channelled by Tony Neate and Diane Furlong. Pegasus Foundation, 1992

The Link: The Extraordinary Gifts of a Teenage Psychic, Matthew Manning. Smythe, 1974

Living Magically: A New Vision of Reality, Gill Edwards. Piatkus, 1991

Living Your Dreams, Gayle Delaney. Harper & Row, 1988

The Lure and Romance of Alchemy, C. J. S. Thompson. Bell Publishing.

Magic and the Magician, W. E. Butler. Aquarian, 1991

The Master Book of Herbalism, Paul Beyerl. Phoenix, 1984

Mediums and their Work, Linda Williamson. Robert Hale, 1992

Mediumship Made Simple, Ivy Northage. Psychic Press, 1990

Meetings with Angels: A Hundred and One Real-life Encounters, H. C. Moolenburgh. C. W. Daniel, 1992

Messengers of Light: The Angels' Guide to Spiritual Growth, Terry Lynn Taylor. H. J. Kramer, 1990

Millennium: Tribal Wisdom and the Modern World, David Maybury Lewis. Viking, 1992

Mind & Magic: An Illustrated Encyclopedia of the Mysterious and Unexplained, Francis X. King. Crescent Books, 1991

Mind to Mind, Betty Shine. Corgi, 1989

Mind Waves, Betty Shine. Corgi, 1994

The 3 Minute Meditator: 30 Simple Ways to Relax and Unwind, David Harp with Nina Feldman. Piatkus, 1992

The Mirror Within: A New Look at Sexuality, Anne Dickson. Quartet Books, 1985

A Modern Herbal, Mrs Grieve. Penguin, 1980

More Lives than One? Jeffrey Iverson. Pan Books, 1976

Mysteries of the Mind, Edgar Cayce. Aquarian, 1990

The Mystical Qabalah, Dion Fortune. Aquarian 1987; first published 1935

Mythical Monsters: Fact or Fiction, Charles Gould. Studio Editions, 1992

Natural Magic, Marian Green. Element, 1989

Natural and Supernatural: A History of the Paranormal, Brian Inglis. Prism Unity, 1992

Occult Exercises and Practices: Gateways to the Four Worlds of Occultism, Gareth Knight. Aquarian, 1982

On Dreams: True-life Examples of Dream Interpretation, Harmon H. Bro. Aquarian, 1989

On Mysteries of the Mind: the Unlimited Scope of Human Consciousness, Edgar Cayce. Aquarian, 1990

The Opening of the Third Eye, Douglas Baker. Aquarian, 1977

Out of Body Experiences: How Science is Helping us to Understand the Experience of Living beyond the Body, Janet Lee Mitchell. Turnstone, 1985

Out on a Limb, Shirley MacLaine. Bantam Books, 1983

Pagan Celtic Britain, Anne Ross. Constable, 1992

The Pagan Religions of the Ancient British Isles: Their Nature and Legacy, Ronald Hutton. Basil Blackwell, 1991

Palmistry for All, Cheiro. D. B. Taraporevala Ltd, 1985

Pendulum Power: A Mystery You Can See, a Power You Can Feel, Greg Nielsen and Joseph Polansky. Aquarian, 1986

People of the Lie: The Hope for Healing Human Evil, M. Scott Peck. Arrow Books, 1990

Personal Mythology: The Psychology of your Evolving Self, David Feinstein and Stanley Krippner. Unwin Paperbacks, 1989

The Power of Myth, Joseph Campbell. Doubleday, 1987

Practical Celtic Magic, Murry Hope. Aquarian, 1987

Practical Guide to the Qabalistic Symbolism, Gareth Knight. Kahn & Averil Press, 1990

Practical Palmistry: A Positive Approach from a Modern Perspective, David Brandon-Jones. CPCS Publications, 1981

The Practice of Personal Transformation: A Workbook for Inner Growth, Strephon Kaplan Williams. Aquarian, 1986

The Presence of the Past: Morphic Resonance and the Habits of Nature, Rupert Sheldrake. Collins, 1988

The Psychic Energy Workbook: An Illustrated Course in Practical Psychic Skills, R. Michael Miller and Josephine M. Harper. Aquarian, 1987

Psychics, Prophets and Mystics: Receiving Information from Paranormal Sources, Jon Klimo. Aquarian, 1991

Psychic Self-Defence: A Study in Occult Pathology and Criminality, Dion Fortune. Aquarian, 1988

Psychic Self-Defence and Well-being, Melita Denning and Osborne Phillips. Llewellyn, 1993

Psychic Sense: Training and Developing Psychic Sensitivity, Mary Swainson and Louisa Bennett. Llewellyn, 1990

Random Acts of Kindness, The Editors of Conari Press. Conari Press, 1993

The Real World of Fairies, Dora van Gelder. Theosophical Publishing House, 1977

The Religion of the Ancient Celts, J. A. MacCulloch. Constable, 1991

Sacred Times: A New Approach to Festivals, William Bloom. Findhorn Press, 1990

Seth Speaks, Jane Robert. Bantam Books, 1974

The Shaman and the Magician, Nevill Drury. Routledge & Kegan Paul, 1982

A Soul's Journey, Peter Richelieu. Aquarian, 1989

The Spiral Dance, Starhawk. Harper & Row, 1979

The Spirits' Book, Allan Kardec. Trubner Press, 1875

The Spiral of Life: Cycles of Reincarnation, Mona Rolfe. C. W. Daniel, 1992

Spiritual Healing: Energy Medicine for Today, Jack Angelo. Element, 1991

Spiritual Realisation: Inner Values in Everyday Life I Chan, Ivy Northage. Pilgrim Books, 1987

Stepping into the Magic: A New Approach to Everyday Life, Gill Edwards. Piatkus, 1993

Story of the Soul, W. H. Church. ARE Press, 1989

Subtle Body: Essence and Shadow, David T. Tansley. Thames & Hudson, 1984

The Tao of Pooh, Benjamin Hoff. Penguin, 1972

The Tarot, Madeleine Montalban. Javelin Books, 1985

The Tibetan Book of the Dead, trans. by Francesca Fremantle and Chogyam Trungpa. Shambhala Dragon Editions, 1987

Time: Rhythm and Repose, Marie Louise von Franz. Thames & Hudson, 1978

The Tree of Life: Symbol of the Centre, Roger Cook. Thames & Hudson, 1974

To Hell with Dying, Alice Walker. Hodder & Stoughton, 1991

The Truth Vibrations, David Icke. Aquarian, 1992

UFOs and How to See Them, Jenny Randle. Anaya, 1993

The Unbelievers: Inside the Supernatural, Jean Ritchie. Fontana, 1992

Vampires, Burial and Death, Paul Barber. Yale University Press, 1988

The Virago Book of Fairy Tales, edited by Angela Carter. Virago, 1990

Water Divining and Other Dowsing: A Practical Guide, Ralph Whitlock. David & Charles, 1982

What Number Are You? Your Numbers and Your Life, Lilla Bek and Robert Holden. Aquarian, 1992

A Witch Alone: Thirteen Moons to Master Natural Magic, Marian Green. Aquarian, 1991

Witchcraft, Pennethorne Hughes. Penguin Books, 1970

What the Buddha Taught, Walpola Rahula. Wisdom Press, 1990

Whole in One, David Lorimer. Arkana, 1990

Of Wolves and Men, Barry Holstun Lopez. Charles Scribner's Sons, 1978

The Woman's Encyclopedia of Myths and Secrets, Barbara G. Walker. Harper & Row, 1983

The Women's Press Book of New Myth and Magic, edited by Helen Windrath. Women's Press, 1993

The Women's Spirituality Book, Diane Stein. Llewellyn, 1987

The World Atlas of Divination, edited by John Matthews. Eddison Sadd, 1992

The World of Buddhism, H. Bechert and E. Gombrich. Thames & Hudson, 1980

You Can Heal Your Life, Louise M. Hay. Eden Grove, 1990

Zen: Direct Pointing to Reality, Anne Bancroft. Thames and Hudson, 1979

Zen and the Art of Motorcycle Maintenance, Robert Pirsig. Bodley Head, 1974

Zen Philosophy, Thich Thien An. DHARMA, 1975

Other Virago UPSTARTS

THE YOUNG PERSON'S ACTION GUIDE TO ANIMAL RIGHTS

Barbara James

Countless animals die every day in abattoirs, experiments, traps, nets, by guns, and by neglect. Where do we draw the line if we care about animals?

Do we refuse veal but eat beef? Become vegetarian but wear leather? Willingly take a new medicine if it has not been tested on animals first? In order to make our minds up about what we really think, we must know the facts. Angling, badger-baiting, circuses, dolphins, genetic engineering, factory farming, hunting, slaughter, vivisection, warfare and more than a hundred more related topics are covered here in a simple A to Z format with up-to-date information and statistics. And at the end of every topic are answers to that important question: *What can you do?*

THE YOUNG PERSON'S GUIDE TO SAVING THE PLANET

Debbie Silver and Bernadette Vallely

All you ever wanted to know about the environment but didn't know who to ask, where to look, what to do . . .

Acid rain, batteries, beauty, CFCs, deodorants, E numbers, the greenhouse effect, hamburgers, noise, the ozone layer, rainforests, television, whales . . . over one hundred environmental issues are all here in a simple A–Z format. But that's only the beginning. This is the first book that shows you what action *you* can take, ranging from small life changes to ways of encouraging family, friends, schools, supermarkets – even industry and governments – to go green. Saving the planet is a tall order. But it's our only world and our only chance. You could make a difference.

TAKE A FIRM STAND
The Young Woman's Guide to Self-defence
Vicky Grosser, Gaby Mason and Rani Parmar

With techniques based on the Kaleghl Quinn method of self-defence for women – here is the first book of its kind especially for young women

The authors of this wonderful book show that a strong sense of self-worth and a basic understanding of self-defence techniques help build your confidence and your ability to look after yourself. This key guide provides you with step-by-step photographs and instructions illustrating fifteen techniques, including effective ways to escape arm grabs and strangleholds. Equal attention is given to non-physical precautionary measures that will reduce the chances of attack.

This essential handbook, dedicated to making your life less restricted and more enjoyable, includes a series of young womens' own success stories, along with information about the law and a list of useful contacts.

HOW DO I LOOK?

Jill Dawson

'I don't think it's dead vain to care about how you look. It's about trying to be an individual, to be noticed, to say: look at me' – Janet

'Some days I'm happy, others I'm not . . . is it to do with my lipstick or my attitude? The sad part is I've come to hate my body so much, I blame it for everything . . .' – Helen

Here young women talk about how they feel about their changing bodies, dressing to make a statement, challenging stereotypes. They speak of longing to be beautiful, of restrictions, and of all-pervasive media images. At a time in life when self-image is intricately woven with feelings about sexuality and identity, here's what young women honestly feel when they look in the mirror, and ask that fascinating, vexing question: how do I look?

LOVE TALK
A Young Person's Guide To Sex, Love and Life
Eleanor Stephens
With cartoons by *Jonathan Bairstow*

Sex, love and all that stuff can be fun, exciting, enthralling and, for teenagers, a minefield. Each generation has had its own problems, double standards, social mores and choices, but the current generation has all that – and AIDS.

Firmly believing that once they have information that is accurate and accessible, young people are capable of handling the powerful changes and important choices that characterise this period, Eleanor Stephens and Jonathan Bairstow have produced an invaluable book to help young people in life and love.

Contents:
Body Talk · Mind Talk · Sex Talk
The First Time · Safe Loving
Birth Control · Who Am I?
Coping With Love · How Do I Look?
Baby Talk · Health Check
Sex-Related Diseases · Sex And
The Law · Jealousy · Friendship

OUT IN THE OPEN
A Guide For Young People Who Have Been Sexually Abused
Ovanié Bain and Maureen Sanders

'The most surprising thing for me was to find out that it wasn't some weird thing that happened just to me'

If you have ever experienced any kind of sexual abuse, this book is for you. Plain-speaking and sympathetic, it cuts through the terrible loneliness and silence and talks frankly about the range of feelings sexually abused young people experience. Including other people's stories and discussing honestly what can happen once the truth is told, it also offers practical advice and encouragement to young people on the road to recovery. Ultimately this is an optimistic books arguing and believing that despite the pain, anger, fears and setbacks, once things are out in the open, victims *can* become survivors.